MADE IN BRIGHTON

MADE IN BRIGHTON

From the Grand to the Gutter: Modern Britain as seen from beside the sea

Julie Burchill and Daniel Raven

This edition published in Great Britain in 2008 by
Virgin Books Ltd
Thames Wharf Studios
Rainville Road
London
W6 9HA

1 3 5 7 9 10 8 6 4 2

First published in hardback in Great Britain in 2007 by Virgin
Books Ltd

A catalogue record for this book is available from the
British Library.

ISBN 978 0 7535 1352 1

Typeset by TW Typesetting, Plymouth, Devon

Printed and bound in Great Britain by
CPI Bookmarque Ltd, Croydon, CR0 4TD

CONTENTS

For Susan Raven

PREFACE BY JULIE BURCHILL

People in Brighton are the most positive and feel the luckiest of any town or city in the UK, according to a survey by the National Lottery.

The city topped the poll, with 93% of residents asked considering themselves lucky.

'We were not surprised. Anyone going to Brighton cannot ignore the buzz,' said psychologist Linda Papodopoulos. 'It is no surprise residents are in such a positive frame of mind.'

August 2006, BBC News

Like Las Vegas, Brighton seems to be in, but not of, the country where it physically resides; a domestic, kiss-me-quick mirage, almost, conjured up when people need a place to go to do things they think they shouldn't. And as Vegas seems physically improbable – a metropolis built on the junction of three deserts – so Brighton in its genteel, miniature manner seems to be hidden from the censorious gaze of 'real life', though only fifty minutes from the capital. To ride on the express from Victoria is to experience this;

the shabby streets and then the suburbs fall away and all seems green and pleasant until – WHOOSH! – you go through a tunnel and come out the other side, pulling into Sodom-on-Sea.

What happens in Brighton stays in Brighton. Except it doesn't. Brighton has become a model village version of Britain, with all of its virtues – good humour, creativity, drunkenness – and its vices – snobbishness, smugness, drunkenness – writ large. It stands alone both of all this island's coastal resorts, and of its Home Counties' retreats, as a place where people go not to escape the excesses of our landlocked cities but to drown in them. Whether through the historic pursuit of extracurricular sex, of the drugs which make it the most likely place to die of an overdose (more so even than London or Glasgow!), or of the cult of youth, which makes Brighton statistically the most stressful place for women to live (while yet strangely the *Grazia* body map survey of Britain found Brighton women happiest with their bodies; 43 per cent totally happy with their weight, while 6 out of 10 will willingly eat a whole packet of biscuits in one go), this is a city by the sea where the picture-postcard prettiness hides a teeming sewer of splendid sleaze and savage amusement.

A word about a word; when I say 'Brighton' I am actually referring, technically, to the City of Brighton and Hove, as it has been since April Fools' Day 1997, when the two towns became one – not so much in the style of devoted Siamese Twins, though, but more as a particularly obdurate Pushme-Pullyu. I was going to say that the merger was 'resented', but really this only cut one way in that it was resented by Hovians; it's fair to say that Brightonians didn't pay it an awful lot of mind – their collective thoughts were probably on more pressing matters, such as what a perfectly *vile* hangover they had, or that *divine* little number they had a hot date with. This is admittedly a typical Hovian view of Brightonians, but there is a basis in truth there; it's as if the suburb which The Monkees sang about in 'Pleasant Valley Sunday' had been slapped down right bang next to Sodom and Gomorrah.

Brighton is a big brassy broad of a town – the sort of broad who wears so much slap that people start to wonder if she's actually a tranny – even with the endless attempts of the lame-brain council to rebrand it as a fully fledged if far-flung branch of deadly dull, good-taste, Euro-portion café society. And as they say, nothing grows in the shade. Anything that Brighton touches comes away smelling of it, and thus not only Hove but also the even more westerly hoods of Southwick, Portslade and Shoreham (where Norman Cook, so totally identified as a Brightonian, actually lives) have been swallowed up by the magnificent beast; you could be forgiven for thinking that Brighton stretches all the way to Worthing these days. This has led Hove in particular to glory in a sort of negative identity vis-à-vis Brighton: Brighton young/Hove old, Brighton gay/Hove straight, Brighton hell-raising/Hove basket-hanging. Buildings in particular have become a battlefield, with Brighton's colourful jumble of Regency beauties and modernistic tower blocks seen by Hovians as a sure sign of anarchic tendencies. In response the more uptight citizens of Hove are fanatically engaged in opposing the demolition of the most ordinary or even unsightly houses – 'family houses', as they are invariably called by their fetishistic protectors, in order, one presumes, to differentiate them from the gay flats and bestiality-bound bedsits which seek to usurp them.

This stick-in-the-mud tendency has the unfortunate effect of making Hove Fundamentalists seem anti-fun in all its forms, and the deeper you go into Hove the worse it gets. One sweltering Sunday afternoon in the summer of 2006, my husband and I set out on a walk along the seafront – but rather than turning left at the Peace Statue and strolling into Brighton, we turned right and walked for half an hour along Hove seafront – past the lawns, past the bathing huts – and, it seemed, right back into the past. When we turned up one of the streets that led off the seafront, it was like walking into another world, or, rather, into an old pop song or sci-fi novel, and not an altogether pleasant one at that. While just up the road Brighton was doing a pretty good imitation of Rio during the Carnival if some mad scientist had seen fit to drop a ton of ground-down Pro Plus into the water supply, here the silent, empty streets had a distinct feel of 'Everyone's Gone To The Moon' or *The Day of the Triffids*. Sure there was no rubbish and no raised voices, no public drunkenness or pubic displays – but neither were there any people, any taxis or any sign of life. In fact it looked *exactly* like the sort of depressed suburb that people run away to Brighton to escape from. Well, they don't have far to go!

Don't get me wrong, I like a bit of quiet – but this was *beyond*. This was the call of the coffin, the tranquillity of the tomb – and it made me totally understand a bit of strange legalese in the contract for a gorgeous flat on Hove seafront which I had recently nixed at the last moment; the mysterious 'Clause Of Quiet Enjoyment'. I mean, fair play – but I've never enjoyed myself quietly in my life, and I don't intend to start now. As we limped footsore towards the sounds, smells and good old life-affirming seediness of Brighton, I couldn't help but think of the excellent Terry Garoghan's *Brighton: The Musical* – specifically his cheeky little number 'Hovogue', performed to the tune of Madonna's 'Vogue':

All around everywhere you go it's quiet
And everybody is old
The streets are full of pussycats
And everybody is DEAD FUCKING OLD

Hove – old biddies wearing bri nylon blouses!
Hove! – yes, HOVE, dear!
Everybody's kicking the bucket!

They're stuck up
They're well bred
They've got orthopaedic beds!

But back to basics: Brighton by any other name. Growing up, and all through my salad days in fact, I was never what you could call an Outdoor Girl. As an adolescent, even the popular makeup range of that name had me shuddering with Draculesque distaste and slouching towards the sludgy salvation of the Biba counter. Born jagged with sophistication and paler than putty, you could pick any summer out of my first sixteen and you'd have found me shut away for the full six weeks of school holiday in my Bristol back bedroom with the curtains firmly closed. Occasionally I'd take my nose out of a thoroughly unsuitable and eye-wateringly pretentious turn-of-the-century novel – in translation, *naturellement* – to poke it through said drapes and press it against the sizzling window pane to stare at the sun. 'Make it go *away!*' I'd whine pitifully before returning to the gripping gripes of some French fag with an interesting disease.

In the hottest summer of the century, that of 1976, I took myself off to London in search of fame, fortune and a whole new city-full of buildings in which to sulk, lurk and sneer through safely sealed windows at people enjoying the sunshine. 'I hate humans,' I would mutter under my breath before going back to ogle the glorious view in my mirror – a regular fun-packet, I was!

I carried on like this for nearly another twenty years – and then, in 1995, I moved to Brighton. And my life as a sun-worshipper, beach-bum and water-baby began in earnest. I've often been asked if I have any regrets about things I've done in my long and louche life; just one, and that's *wasting so much time stuck indoors when it's lovely out there*! For once, my mother had been right.

But it took a seaside town to change my mind. If I'd stayed in London, I'd still be sulking, lurking and sneering behind closed doors because when the temperature rises in the concrete canyons, it's more than ever a jungle. Italian and Spanish cities handle the heat by taking a siesta; all the Parisians who can afford to simply abandon the city wholesale. (In July and August there are more Frenchies between the ages of 16 and 21 in Brighton than there are in Paris. They tell their parents it's the lure of the language schools; they tell us it's the sex, drugs and clubbing.) But Londoners hang on in there, neither napping nor fleeing, and they get *mad as hell*. You're well better off behind closed doors.

Brighton, of course, comes into its own in the sunshine. It's still beautiful when windswept in the rain, when walking on the esplanade feels like being in a Smiths video and connects one thrillingly with the drenched but undefeated island spirit of our damp, dazzling people. But when the sun comes out, it truly is 'that paradise of brightness' that A.E. Coppard eulogised, and which S.P.B. Mais was thinking of when he stated that: 'Anyone who does not live in Brighton is mad and should be locked up.'

When the sun shines and the temperature rises in Britain, the other Two Nations schism – alongside rich and poor, North and South, town and country – becomes illuminated. The landlocked Britain closes in on its captives; the coastal Britain opens up, up, up, giving the experience of living physically *on the edge* of one's country an almost vertiginous dazzle and shimmer. It's like we're so ... *out there* ... that *anything* could happen. And most Brighton stories, which can variously end up in rooms rented by the hour, painting oneself as a zebra (and meaning it sincerely), or waking up dressed in the garb of the opposite sex on a ferry to Rotterdam, start on the beach.

Strictly speaking, the beach of the City of Brighton & Hove stretches almost three miles from Shoreham to Rottingdean, but the spirit of Brighton Beach resides between the Peace Statue in the west to the Palace Pier in the east. Massive investment has transformed this central mile of beachfront over the past decade; Charlotte Raven, who grew up in Brighton, says:

> When I was a teenager there was nothing on the seafront except places where you could get chips and tea out of polystyrene cups. There was one café under the arches where you could go and shelter from the weather. We mods used to sit there and argue about whose turn it was to go and get more lighter fuel. It was all very seamy and much more atmospheric whereas it feels so much more like London now – same people, same bloody cappuccinos!

Charlotte also called the old neglected seafront 'a wonderful prompt for human narratives' – and looking at the pristine Artists Quarter, Fishing Museum and Volleyball Court, where one's responses are all cued up and ready to go, you could argue that prosperity has been paid for with sheer seedy character. And that this could be a chic, bustling promenade anywhere from Positano to San Francisco, as the beautiful people linger over a latte and plan a hard day's antique shopping.

But I'm nit-picking. When it still feels like an honour to live somewhere after eleven years, how bad can it be? *And it's still so not London!* Beyond the Palace Pier going east towards the Marina, the chill, slick hand of the style police has not yet crushed Brighton's grand tradition of agreeable, ramshackle blowsiness, and you can still ride the quaint Volks Railway past the abandoned Peter Pan's Playground and the desperately dated, utterly adorable 'nudist beach'. Here Little Englander Modernists like me can find the rusty radiance of the resistance to the global village and the Euro-portion which is summed up in the county motto of Sussex: We Won't Be Druv.

The revamps, the facelifts and the attempts by a clumsy council to write the indigenous Brighton working class out of the upwardly mobile picture are real enough. But on the beach, you get the distinct feeling that Brighton will never completely pull its socks up. Already the white-flight London breeders who came here to create a vast Nappy Valley – a kind of Clapham-on-Sea – are appalled by our unparalleled drug-taking (see above OD stat) and assorted high jinks. Even between the piers, where the gentrification is most obvious and where every citizen should in theory be shopping for hand-painted *objets*, the vast dope cloud still rises, like a phoenix in reverse, silently and smilingly refusing to be born-again as an on-message, user-friendly unit of the ongoing British economic miracle which has seen us over the past decade come to work the longest hours in Europe – and along the way become one of its most miserable nations. But time passes so quickly in the blameless, shameless sun, on the eternal beach, where the going out and coming in of the ocean makes the only real sense. A working day can be lost forever in the blink of an eye, in forty winks, in a couple of cans of Stella and a cheeky spliff. And a good thing too.

Living on the edge, *coasting*, can give one a great deal of perspective – dangerous, healthy perspective – in a culture where workers may be underpaid and harassed and discarded in a manner that trade union strength would not have allowed a few decades back. It makes you aware that, when you finally lie dying, you'll never regret your day in the sun. You won't remember your time on the beach as time wasted; instead, you'll look back bitterly at all that time behind sealed windows, pushing paper and kissing butt, when the sun was – finally! – shining as the precious days you frittered away. And if I ever fret momentarily as I tug at my Miraclesuit and turn on my front to even up my tan, and ask myself if I really shouldn't go inside and start working now, the breezy, easy brother of Jiminy Cricket, who sits on the shoulder of every warm-blooded Brightonian, leans close and whispers, 'It'll keep . . .'

If you still show an unhealthy desire to put nose to grindstone, shoulder to wheel, or to indulge in any other such self-loathing and anatomically outlandish stunts, he will most likely see fit to remind you that when you were a child, at the end of a day by the seaside, when your parents dragged you back to real, landlocked, boring life, you could barely get your head around the fact that *some people didn't have to leave – because they lived there, all the time*!

Now I am one of those maddeningly jammy dodgers. I've been here in Brighton for twelve years, and the weird thing is that in the best possible way it still doesn't feel like home. Instead it feels like I somehow got out of going home – time and time and time again – and that I escaped from the life that had been mapped out for me in the landlocked limbo of London; the slo-mo, stressed-out, wound-down fatalism of growing up and growing old. Now *that's* lucky, if you like.

January 2007

PREFACE BY DANIEL RAVEN

At eight years old I too dreamed of escaping from London. I hated school, where I had hardly any friends on account of sounding 'posh', I wasn't allowed out on my own in case I got kidnapped by prostitutes (at least that's what I assumed the threat was – and why else would anyone spend half an hour walking around our block, visibly trying not to look suspicious?) and there was nowhere to buy American comics, or indeed anything else of interest, because this was Streatham. It probably wasn't any grimmer than anywhere else in outer London at the dawn of the 1980s, but all my memories of the place are underscored by a low hum of constant background mankiness: peeling flyposters on every wall, National Front graffiti on every lamppost, 'I Don't Like Mondays' on every bleeding radio . . .

I knew I didn't want to be there, but typically assumed everywhere else would be just the same, if not a good deal worse; my school in Streatham was depressing, certainly, but to switch to a new one would surely be to invite *Grange* Hill-style swimming pool tragedies. I sobbed and sulked all the way down the M23 until finally we arrived in Brighton – and, actually, it was fine. Our new house was just around the corner from Preston Park, which was as beautiful then as it is now, and my new school was manageably sized and friendly, with the expected jibes about my accent never materialising (it seemed I'd never really been posh at all – just *desperately* middle class, darling!). Perhaps best of all, there was a science fiction bookshop on the other side of the park – Vortex Books – which sold *all* the American comics *at least two months in advance of their cover dates*, and although the bearded man who ran it clearly disliked children, he'd still let you buy stuff!! It was almost more than my tiny heart could stand.

That said, central Brighton in 1981 bore little resemblance to the squeaky-clean, kooky stationery lovers' Mecca we know today – here too was mankiness. The conference trade was booming and the town was already attracting upwards of 35,000 language students a year, but revenue from your actual holidaymakers had dropped sharply and evidence of the recession was everywhere (except Preston Park). The lower esplanade of the seafront, now teeming with cafés, bars and galleries, was then an eerie strip of near-Eastbourneian emptiness, punctuated only by a dingy arcade, a handful of boarded-up rock shops and the occasional notorious toilet. Churchill Square was not the sterile, identikit indoor mall we presently plod through but a grimy, baffling[1] outdoor one bristling with empty units. The Marina – whose attractions now include a huge hotel, an equally vast supermarket, a casino, a multiplex cinema, a string of bars, restaurants and even places to *live* – was just a Marina. A half-empty Marina.

---

[1] Baffling how? Well, it may have been built in the days before psychology had anything to do with marketing but it's still hard to imagine anyone saying, 'Ah yes, we'll build the whole thing from great slabs of concrete – syphilis grey, for the ages! The centrepiece will be a mighty stone tower in the Aztec style, designed with the lavatorial requirements of seabirds very much in mind yet easily scaleable by all but the smallest infant, with a serene garden of jagged rocks surrounding its base. And finally, to demonstrate that our Centre is proud to be a part of *modern* Brighton, there will be a bridge leading directly to the top floor of the Brighton (Conference) Centre – and a security guard to make sure no one ever uses it!' Listen to me being snotty, though – at the time I'd never even seen a shopping centre before, and thought Churchill Square was the *coolest*. Trying to sneak past that security guard was often the highlight of my week.

But! We had the North Laines. If Brighton were a pair of jeans (with leather chaps, natch), the North Laines would be the condom pocket – indisputably central yet curiously easy to disregard, with a tendency to secrete forgotten treasures. Cradled in the right angle of London Road and North Street and adjoining the train station to the west, they nonetheless remain hidden from the casual shopper (who in any case may only be seeking big name high street action) or tourist (unlikely to wander east from the station when the sea can clearly be seen to the south). Their uniquely indeterminate situation gave – and, to some extent, still gives – them a uniquely unruly atmosphere; in those days, the whole area looked like the outer fringes of a music festival that had gone on so long all the traders had managed to build houses around their stalls without once letting the bongs go out. I was about fourteen when I first started hanging around there, and just naïve enough to think I'd stumbled upon the 'real' Brighton.

Delights abounded: second-hand record shops run by bearded men who clearly disliked teenagers (generally a bit fatter than the bloke from Vortex, though, and with dazed-looking, dreadlocked lieutenants), second-hand bookshops (principally David's Book Exchange, whose proprietor[2] had the avuncular-if-grasping air of a mildly offensive Jewish stereotype from an early 70s sitcom and was rumoured to have a bath full of urine upstairs), second-hand clothes shops (like Uncle Sam's Vintage American, where Jean-Yves the camp Frenchman used to work before he started stoogeing for Jim Davidson on TV's *The Generation Game*), Vegetarian Shoes (Vegetarian Shoes!) and the Jubilee Shopping Hall, a flea market that looked like it thought it was a department store (the entire first floor was empty apart from one small poster shop – *unthinkable* on Gardner Street today). I'd never seen places or people like this before but they all seemed to make perfect sense, inasmuch as you knew they would have made no sense at all anywhere else. Dog-eared pubs like the Prince George

---

[2] Sadly no longer with us, though his splendid shop remains.

and the Green Dragon would nightly be stormed by a hundred and one varieties of fruitcake, all with their own confusingly original theories about politics, history and/or the creative talents with which they would shortly stun the world; goths, punks, hippies, mods and teds – yes, teds! – would laugh, argue, or try to start bands with them. Fittingly, the only street sign[3] to formally identify this strange land had been misspelled, 'Welcome to the North Laine Conversation Area'. And if you didn't like conversation, there was always the Dorset Arms.

The Dorset was a classic old man's pub – peeling plaster, broken jukebox, cloudy horse brasses – but they seemed to be running a little short on old men. It was profoundly empty almost every night and the stench of defeat hung heavily in the air, just under the banner proclaiming, 'The Party's Here!' that no one had ever had the energy to remove. Sometimes there'd be a DJ, which is to say an elderly, bespectacled record collector with a box of Gene Vincent 7"s and a Dansette who closed his every engagement with Ivor Biggun's 'I'm a Wanker', but for the most part it was all about staring at walls in total silence.

Me and my friends ended up spending a lot of time there, because you could always get a seat and the bar staff always looked pleased to see you; we may even have experienced misplaced feelings of ownership towards it. When it closed down and reopened as 'The Dorset Street Bar', flogging fancy bottled lagers, sun-blushed tomato ciabattas and fucking *coffee* of all things, it seemed to us hilariously inappropriate – 'the Dorset *what* bar?' 'The Dorset Street *what?*' – but, in hindsight, we sniggered too soon. Big changes were afoot in Brighton, changes that would threaten to make old men of us all – and in my case, if we're honest, succeed.

Apparently London was starting to look a bit small, or at least all the nice bits of it were, and a whole generation of wealthy young professionals and dropouts was finding itself distinctly underwhelmed by the prospect of forking out silly zlotys just to

---

[3] At the corner of Frederick Street and Gloucester Road, fact fans!

get a big, boring house in Hampstead like its parents'. These people were keen to strike out, to make a statement, to be individuals, separately but at the same time – and what better place to do all that than Brighton, celebrated home of the 'alternative lifestyle'? Many were also spawning, and anxious to remove their young from the pernicious influence of the big, bad city that had made them rich; they liked Brighton because it was safer than London while also being more like London than anywhere else that was that close to London.

They all loved their new seaside homes and showed off about them to their friends, who duly began to wonder if there might be a pebble-shaped hole in their own lives. (So what if they had to be in town most of the week? There was nothing to stop them getting a little place for weekends, and it'd be a great investment too!) The result was that, from 1999 onwards, property prices in Brighton skyrocketed. Landlords all over town drastically increased their rents or sold up completely; dozens of office buildings were converted into posh apartment blocks. Suddenly, people who had always belonged to Brighton could no longer afford to live there: not just the North Laines fruitcakes but teachers, firemen, nurses. Web designers poured in to replace them – and if there's one thing web designers like, it's coffee.

As a nation we are often encouraged to laugh at, or be shamed by, the absurdity of working-class English holidaymakers who go to Spain and insist on eating pie and chips every day, yet when these incoming Londoners (most of whom wouldn't dream of going on that sort of holiday) began to remake Brighton in Islington's image, no one in authority seemed anything but grateful. Today, the North Laines area is a shiny shadow of its former self. Some of the old shops and people are still there, but they're increasingly crowded out by smug coffee chains and ponceoid boutiques. The Prince George now refers to itself as 'George' and the Green Dragon has become – wait for it – 'Office'.

Don't get me wrong: I actually quite like fancy bottled lagers and ciabatta, even warm goats' cheese salad. And I've nothing against places that look clean and smart: leather sofas, spider plants, bit of chrome on the tables, bit of art on the walls ... But when everywhere you go has all of these things and not much else, it's amazing how quickly you can start to yearn for sticky carpets and soggy beer mats, even Ivor Biggun.

Of course, this is a pretty petty gripe next to those of the outgoing teachers, firemen and nurses; for anyone who can still afford to live in Brighton or Hove,[4] they're still very nice places to live. And maybe, if we apply even more perspective, it isn't actually worth making such a fuss about. That old chestnut the Shock of the New has, after all, had more than its share of previous in this vicinity, and, generally speaking, things have always turned out for the best. When Dr Richard Russell published his *Glandular Diseases, or a Dissertation on the Use of Sea Water in Affections of the Glands* in 1750, a poverty-stricken fishing village of less than 500 households called Brighthelmston was besieged by rich and fashionable visitors seeking a dunk in its healing waters. The level of culture shock experienced by its indigenous workers must have been staggering but they adapted, offering boat rides and rooms for lodging, taking jobs in the new hotels and on the seafront as 'dippers' (literally, the ones who did the dunking), or plying any or all of a whole host of less reputable trades. They adapted so well, in fact, that 46 years later Brighton's dolphin emblem was described in a London newspaper as 'a shark that lives on gold'.

When the train station opened in 1841 the invasion was stepped up a gear: 75,000 trippers arrived every week in the summer of 1850, compared to 25,000 *a year* in the days before the railway. The town's more prosperous residents and visitors were naturally aghast at the heightened level of working-class shoulder-rubbing this entailed, and formed conservation groups to oppose anything that threatened to attract any more of the bothersome oiks – the West Pier, for instance. They too were

---

[4] Not, as we are now encouraged to say, 'Brighton *and* Hove', because that would be stupid. How can you live in Brighton *and* Hove?

forced to adapt (mainly, one suspects, by moving to Hove), and a little over a hundred years later the descendants of those same groups were campaigning for the pier's preservation.

That's what I'll do, then: I'll adapt. Hey, I'm trying![5] I certainly don't mind being part of the shark that lives on gold, if indeed that is what we're doing this time. The truth is there is not, nor has there ever been, a 'real' Brighton to defend, unless you count that poverty-stricken eighteenth-century fishing village: it has always been a mosaic of clashing cultures and conflicting interests, and all the better for it. What's important is the scrum itself, and throwing yourself into it, and making sure you're still conscious at the end to see who won.

As of this writing, property prices in Brighton have failed to rise significantly since 2004. Just, you know, 'FYI' . . .

---

[5] I even work for a web design company . . .

YOU CAN'T DRY YOUR NETS HERE
ANY MORE

The story of the Brighton working class is no day in the sun, but rather a long and exhausting water-tread in the meagre margins of the shallow end – forever treated not as an essential part of The Place To Be's much-trumpeted 'diversity' but rather as a dirty great Burberry-clad burden on the sleek, mobile, modern, clean machine that is B&H. The feeling of our Great And The Good – who in my experience might be more accurately described as the Mediocre And The Mean – that the proletariat somehow 'get in the way' of, as opposed to completely and kindly facilitate, the fabulousness of our fantastic seaside playpen is extreme here. Far more so than in London, to give the capital credit for once, which does to some extent acknowledge the crucial part its poorest people have always played in its creation, growth and culture. Here, Let Them Eat Rock seems to be the considered reaction to the plight of the poor. Indeed, a few years back, when the Brighton *Argus* drew attention to the fact that thousands of local nurses, bin-men and firefighters were living on the breadline, and that they found it well nigh impossible to buy even modest homes in the city their work healed, cleaned and saved, a prominent friend of the council spoke the immortal words, 'Oh, put them all in Hastings and build a monorail!' In short, let disease, plague rats and pyromaniacs do their worst – Man can, and will, live off polenta and wi-fi access alone!

It was ever thus, beside the seaside; specifically, at the Brighton seaside, where the wages of the working class are the lowest in the whole of the South East and, according to May 2006 figures from the Office for National Statistics, the rate of unemployment is the highest in the region – at 6.4 per cent, compared with a regional figure of 5.4 and a national figure of just 3.7. Erosion of the indigenous industry could be traced back as far as 1799, when some sticky-beaked snoot-bag wrote of the rectangle of greenery that faces the Royal Pavilion, 'Fishing nets are daily spread from one end of the Steine to another, so that company while walking are frequently tripped up by entangling their feet.' This was a reference to the displeasure felt by incoming London toffs who, amazingly, arrived in a coastal town to find its people engaged in the outrageous business of earning a living by catching fish, the shameless, smelly cads! And so in the early 1820s railings were erected around the Steine and the fishermen forced to stop the age-old practice of drying their nets there; a striking illustration of the monumentally warped notion – still held to this day by some – that the sight of people going about the business of working for a living is somehow *more* offensive than the sight of parasites on parade, be they Charles Windsor lecturing us about the future of the planet, the Queen riding in a solid gold carriage to give the world's oldest parliamentary democracy the OK, or, indeed, a bunch of jumped-up bean-counters running around piercing churches and believing that this somehow qualifies a 'hood to be European City of Culture. Forget fish-guts – that's the sort of stink that turns any right-minded cove's stomach.

So – a town built around a playboy prince's pleasure palace, stripped of its native industry and railroaded into sucking up to visiting snobs on the grand scale in order to make a living; it seems nothing if not predictable that the working class of Brighton and Hove ended up with the sticky end of the lollipop. When it comes to the legendary 'diversity' of this town, they truly are the invisible legions. If you're a gay or a tranny, a bi or a lezzer, a recent immigrant or an established businessman, the path to your door will be worn quite smooth by the council fusspots who have been beating it in a ceaseless frenzy to hear your complaints, suggestions and demands. But the only reason they ever seem to bother to call on the white working class is to attempt to persuade them to up sticks and move elsewhere – Wales, Manchester and Milton Keynes have all been mooted, though few Brightonians have felt the pull of these faraway places with strange-sounding names.

Still, it doesn't exactly make folk feel . . . wanted, as it were. Anyway, even if they didn't accept the proffered postcode-changing carrot, it looked as though Brighton was going to rid itself of its altogether pesky key workers – neither use nor ornament, m'dear! – one way or another. In December 2005, under the headline EXODUS, the *Argus* predicted that soaring house prices would force some 10,000 families, a good number of them headed by nurses, teachers, firefighters and police (you know, all those frivolous, outmoded, unnecessary trades), to leave B&H over the coming three years. The average property price had risen to £219,000 – more than eight times the average salary of £25,000, and far beyond the 3.5 x salary that banks are up for lending. What's more, a dirty great 60 per cent of all households earn less than the £29,000 income required to buy even the cheapest homes here – and, chillingly, every fire service employee surveyed fitted into this category. What a strange paradox, that the very people who would be called upon to save the dream homes of rich incoming London professionals – my good self included – from fiery destruction may soon be forced to flee the city that will beg them to save it, for the searing, simple reason that they cannot afford to put even a modest roof over their own heads! As Mark Turner of B&H GMB union pointed out, 'If people are leaving because they cannot afford the cost of housing within the city, it will have a catastrophic effect on the provision of public services.'

A little anecdote here, combining two of my favourite things: standing up for the workers, and making a truckload of cash without even trying. As luck would have it, I was already doing my bit for more affordable housing for key workers. 'Do good by doing good' is one of my rules of life – along with 'Teach fun' and 'When in doubt, pout' – so imagine my glee when in the summer of 2004 I inked an agreement to sell my house to a flat-building developer for a cool £1.25 m – a nice round £1 million more than I had bought it for eight years previously. And in the winter of 2004 I found myself on the front page of the *Argus* once more. However, this time I wasn't the ragged Robin Hood of BURCHILL FIGHTS FOR THE TENANTS but rather the swinish Sheriff of Notts fighting off a righteous mob – BURCHILL HITS OUT AS PROTESTERS RING HOUSE – and being portrayed as a moustache-twirling baddy.

Well, they got the first bit right – the price of Immac these days! – but the second bit was way off. Forty per cent of the 78 flats to be built on the sites sold by me and three of my neighbours would go to the very key workers who were in danger of being priced out of the city, while the protesters were more self-righteous than righteous proper; some of them had tried to do a similar deal some months previously, only to see it fall through, which made them not a little cheesed off that we on the sunny side of the street had in fact pulled it off. And actually the two headlines were sister stories under the skin, linked by a common theme: namely, my support for the right of the most important people in Brighton and Hove – the low-paid, actual workers who do the jobs that the city would come to a standstill without – to live in decent housing. The difference was that in the story behind the first headline I'd given money – to Defend Council Housing – and in the second I'd received it – a dashed fine wad from a developer.

The impression I got from the people opposed to the building of 78 flats where once four rambling houses had stood was that it stemmed not from any great love of architecture – I adored my house but, to be frank, it always struck me as an eyesore, and I only bought it for the swimming pool – but rather from a fear and loathing of the 40 per cent of incomers who were perceived as not fitting neatly into the heady heights of the ABC1 demographic so prevalent in that part of Hove. As these were likely to be nurses, bin-men and firefighters, I found this attitude to be particularly repellent, and if I had been wavering over my decision before, these Hyacinth-Bucket-gone-wild antics quickly made my mind up.

As the *Argus* reported it, my house had been 'ringed' by some forty protesters waving placards and carrying banners – this being Hove, of course, they were so damn *quiet* that I didn't know they were there – bearing such elegant, profound legends as FIGHT TO KEEP THE CHARACTER OF BRIGHTON AND HOVE and SAVE OUR FAMILY HOMES. In a delightfully playful response – lost on such clod-hopping lemon-suckers, one presumes – I requested, through the *Argus*, that the most vociferous protesters should volunteer to be wired up to a lie detector ('A proper police one, *not* a toy' – bless!) and asked whether or not they too would sell their property to a developer for several times its market price. If proved wrong, I promised to give a sizeable donation to their KEEP HOVE NOT HORRID campaign, and, just for laffs, to put up a hanging basket outside my house for a day. But if *they* lost, they had to throw off their inhibitions and become born-again Brightonians for a day – reciting a chunk of Modernist poetry on the pier while off their trolley on E and snogging a member of their own gender.

That shut the two-faced yellow-bellied HORRIFIED OF HOVES up pronto, and no mistake!

I also pointed out – piping indignantly no doubt – that the grand-sounding 'Chatsworth Square', behind my house, where many of the geek chorus lived, is also a new development. I quote: 'I had to put up with what looks like Lego Village being built right up against my garden for two years and I didn't complain about the inconvenience as I am mature and unselfish enough to understand people have to live somewhere – even in ugly buildings like Legoland.'

One protester wasn't half so generous: 'Inappropriate developments have become a city-wide problem. There is growing upset among many residents that large developments are not the best way to meet the need for homes for key workers and for affordable housing.'

What would be then? Digging holes in the ground, and praying that the good Lord will see fit to turn the homeless into moles? Of course, 546 of Brighton and Hove's homeless are children, according to Local Authority figures from March 2006, which were quite some way down on Shelter's figure for homeless children in B&H from the previous December – 2,500. And kiddies don't need permanent homes to live in, bless 'em – just give 'em an orange crate and a couple of Wet-Wipes each and their young imaginations can fashion limitless palaces from such raw materials!

Eventually, this protest and other local ones like it – poor Chris Eubank, just a few streets from me, also had the playa-haters on his back something chronic – became so heated that they caught the eye of ITV's *Tonight with Trevor McDonald*. How I purred as a young reporter handed one of my tormentors a shovel, backed away smiling and stood back watching while she dug herself blithely into a hole. The conversation went something like this, as I recall through a drug-addled haze:

> Sweet Young Reporter (gesturing at my erstwhile street, or rather 'avenue', which speaks volumes): 'It's very nice around here, isn't it?'
> Sour Old Nimbyist: 'Yes – and we want to keep it that way!'
> Sweet Young Reporter: 'But wouldn't it be the generous thing to share such a nice neighbourhood with a few more people?'

I don't recall the namby-pamby Nimbyist's answer, probably because I was prancing around the room, punching the air and screeching at the top of my voice. But you get my drift . . .

One of the arguments against this development, and others, is that it will 'destroy community', but I don't remember the liberal middle classes now squealing for things to be forever preserved in aspic having much sympathy with this country's working class when they saw communities they had lived in for hundreds of years altered irretrievably by wave after wave of immigration. Of course, any of them who felt confused and/or resentful about the mutation of their neighbourhoods were ridiculed and/or reviled as 'fascists' by their more educated brethren. But as the brilliant Michael Collins said in his excellent book *The Likes Of Us: A Biography Of The White Working Class*:

Long after the cosy fug of the music hall came the summer haze of Notting Hill's annual Mardi Gras, through which black men and women were viewed by certain middle-class columnists of the left, patronisingly and exclusively, as victims or exotica. It was a view as parochial, and as much the stuff of cliché, as anything the extreme right had come up with when portraying them solely as muggers or murderers, or white society in general when it was rumoured to have them down as minstrels or maids.

Meanwhile, the modern-day white working class had a more varied, more honest, more intimate experience, having known non-whites as lovers, muggers, husbands, killers, wives, victims, neighbours, rapists, friends, foes, attackers, carers. For decades the urban white working class had largely been educated in multiracial schools, worked in multiracial environments, and lived in multiracial neighbourhoods. Many may not have wanted this, and many escaped it in the form of 'white flight', but many more accepted it – or at least didn't manifest their opposition by rioting or carrying out racist attacks.

And now I'm supposed to feel sorry for a bunch of white professionals boo-hooing about all those evil bin-men and nurses – coming here, taking our parking spaces! Honestly, what sort of 'community' worthy of the name wouldn't realise how much the presence of nurses, firefighters and other key workers would enrich it, and what sort of community wouldn't bend over backwards to put out the welcome mat for such everyday heroes? Sadly, I often feel these days that when the word 'community' is uttered it is not used as a jolly invite – community singing! – but rather as a weapon wielded by boorish bigmouths with an axe to grind and not a leg to stand on, be they burning books in Bradford or having hissy fits in Hove.

Anyway, who needed the B-list belly-achers; teachers and nurses said they were delighted at the prospect of affordable housing in such a lush neighbourhood, while a conservationist pointed out that it was far better to build new homes on existing sites than to destroy vast swathes of downs and woodland. A caller to a local radio show summed my critics up best, I feel: 'These people who talk about community being destroyed don't know the meaning of the word. They don't want to be part of a community – they want to sit smugly in their big houses at the end of their long driveways watching the price of their properties go up.'

That I am a better poker player than them is really what gets their goat – that I knew when to hold, fold and walk away from the table; doing good by doing good. And that I have a life which is full and happy enough to allow me to realise that home is where the heart is, that moving on is part of being alive and kicking rather than dead and buried, and that an overly developed attachment to bricks and mortar is really rather sad. I had some brilliant times in my old house, but I saw no reason why fun shouldn't be equally forthcoming in a place with a different postcode. Only slightly different mind you – I like the neighbourhood so much, as it is and as it will be, that I've only moved to the next street; to a dreaded *flat*, no less!

Of course, the Haves seeking to keep the Have Nots at arm's length/spitting distance is nothing new, even in happy-go-lucky, kiss-me-quick Brighton. As my colleague Mr Raven pointed out in his Foreword, as far back as the opening of the train station in 1841, the town's wealthier residents and visitors were having the vapours about the shocking number of their working-class countrymen and women being allowed out of the factories every weekend who dared to take the sea air alongside their betters, leading them to campaign vigorously against such notorious shag-palaces as the West Pier. These days, of course, rather than identify themselves so openly as flaming snobs, they'd merely stay at home and mock the open hearted day-trippers as chavs . . .

Chav: even saying the word seems to me like spitting in the faces of 99.9 per cent of the people I've ever loved. But it's not just a moral objection that's always made me steer clear of the word – vanity plays a big part in it too. And that's not vanity as in fear of being called a chav; on the contrary, I've courted that, with my acutely cute self-description, 'I'm too rich and uneducated to be middle class! *I'm a rich chav!*' No, I mean vanity as in the fact that I've noticed that the one thing this word is good for is that it says so much more about the abuser than the abused. Use of this word says: 'I am extremely disappointed with my life, and I feel that even the most disadvantaged strata of my society is having a far better time than me, despite what I perceive to be their ignorance and unattractiveness.'

Amusingly, when the abuser starts in on exactly what it is that they find so appalling about chavs, it also pinpoints the exact area that the name-caller is most anxious about. Thus, people who aren't getting any good lovin' will hiss ceaselessly on about how slaggy chavs are; those who know that their job is one long duck, dive 'n' skive (usually journalists) will bang on about how idle chavs are; and those who were silly enough to stay in long and expensive educations yet are earning less before tax per annum than Wayne Rooney spends on valet parking each year will be rather cross about how much cash he pulls in with no help from anyone bar his rather clever feet. It's not just individuals; whole groups and institutions can be chav-baiters. Among the leaders here would be the *Daily Mail* (motto: Someone Somewhere Is Having Fun And It Must Be Stopped Now), which goes for the hat trick and gripes about their sex drive, their money and their laziness. (Go figure!)

But I always make a point of standing up for chavs, partly because I'm a rich, idle sex fiend myself, and partly because I find it rather cowardly to insult the one ethnic group – the white working class – which you can safely pick on without feeling the fetid breath of the Commission for Racial Equality on your neck. Quite frankly, it's nothing but social racism – and social racism is as scummy as any other kind. And when I do this, there is always some joker who will bend over backwards attempting to reassure me that not all the working class are wasters. No, there are the good proles, you see (and my dear departed parents were probably amongst them, I am hastily assured – lawks a mussy, thank you, guv, may I get down on my knees and shine your expensive shoes *right now*!), the ones who slave away from cradle to grave ruining their health for a pittance, never speaking until they're spoken to. But then, apparently, there are these bad proles – the chavs – who work no harder than they have to for their minimum wage, and like to spend what little money they have on nice things for themselves and their children; those, in fact, who are sensible and hedonistic and, to their weird detractors (forever fretting about things they themselves can't be/don't have), strangely unashamed of it.

And here's the rub; that the very things that chavs stand accused of – aspiration, love of material goods, lack of communal values – are the *very* things which have not just been fetishised by the likes of the *Daily Mail* for the past thirty years, but forced on the British people as surely as the Industrial Revolution was. The De-Industrial Revolution, started by the *Mail*'s heroine Mrs Thatcher, deprived the working class of skills, trades and neighbourhood socialism, seen most dramatically in the defeat of the miners. Twenty years on, it's a bit late for the genteel voices of the

Establishment to pine for beautiful hand-stitched banners, brass bands and scrubbed doorsteps – that's all gone.

No, we've got to work with what we've got now, and sticky-beaked sad-sacks trying to differentiate between good and bad proles solely on the basis of whether they wear Burberry baseball caps or cloth caps are only displaying their rank ignorance of recent history, as well as their totally transparent and inconceivably sad desire to feel superior to people who have not been dealt the best hand, both educationally and economically speaking, yet still manage to wring a fair amount of fun from life. In the nineteenth century, middle-class do-gooders berated London coster-mongers for spending 'too much' money on nice clothes for their children; nothing changes, except that now the clothes come from Von Dutch. The working class still spend shamelessly – as in 'without shame' – as they rightly should, because which class has worked harder for its money? Perhaps it is their 'betters' who should be more shamefaced in their weird, status-needy spending, be it on five types of extortionately priced organic lettuce, a king's ransom on a fortnight's purgatory in a Tuscany mausoleum, or blowing £300 a throw on having some vicious bint pelt you with hot stones, as many middle-class media madwomen of my acquaintance are apt to do.

Whatever, whenever I hear some well-connected, expensively educated no-mark daring to differentiate between the good/bad and the deserving/undeserving working class, it only has the effect of making me cleave to the bad, 'undeserving' half, out of the pride that is born from knowing that every class has its oiks, yobs and wastrels – Lord Lucan, anyone? the Windsors? – but only the working class, which after all has the most excuse for having them, is publicly pilloried over them. My people! Right, wrong or falling down drunk on WKD with vomit down their velour. And a people so lacking in hypocrisy – very probably the most ludicrous minor vice of all – and so rich in honesty that anyone worthy of the tag human has to like them. 'If we weren't doing this, we'd be on the checkout at Tesco,' says the chav princess Cheryl Cole of the magnificent Girls Aloud. Somehow, I just can't imagine Jade Jagger, or any of the endless, boring Redgrave broads, admitting the same about the benefits of being born with a famous name and no discernible talent.

Anyway, to paraphrase Obi Wan Kenobi, 'Who is the chav – the chav, or the one who disses him?' For websites such as Chavscum demonstrate exactly the mean-mindedness and talent to abuse which chav-haters accuse chavs of. Physician, heal thyself; Nimby, clean up thine own backyard; graceless scum with a mean-minded loathing of your fellow man, put your own stinking website in order!

The chav phenomenon is particularly significant to this book as the original title suggested by the publishers was 'We Are Not Chavs', because of what the Brighton-born, London-dwelling editor saw as a problem bigger in the place she came from than she place she lived in. At first, of course, I flew to my adopted hometown's defence, but there are elements of snobbery here which I have not come across in the dirty old monster up the M23. My London was full of penny-ante, petty-minded media feuds, no doubt – but they were with those in a similar income bracket, with our 'frenemies' in fact; all good sport. In Brighton there are the usual plethora of Mapp-and-Lucia hissy-fits, but I have also come across a spite towards members of other social groups which I did not find at the Groucho Club, where, on the contrary, my friends and I sucked up quite magnificently to the waiting staff, and where people are so obsessed with keeping hold of their cleaners and nannies that they will offer them everything but the promise of bowls of M&Ms with all the brown ones removed by the boss's hand. In London, middle-class professionals who could afford to move out will willingly stay in Brixton and happily chatter about the 'vibrance' of the place, albeit over bursts of gunfire; in Brighton, no one who could afford not to would stay in Whitehawk, though it is a good deal less ugly and violent than its equivalent London estates.

Nor has there ever been, to my knowledge, a Brighton pop song romanticising love-across-the-postcodes in the manner of 'East End boys and West End Girls'. Indeed, a member of one of the town's most garlanded indie bands recently warned readers of the *NME*'s student guide to 'stay away' from West Street, the top choice Saturday night revel-run of Brighton working-class youth since time immemorial or, as he put it, 'Brighton's very own Ibiza strip'. Oooo, wouldn't want anybody to get their ANARCHY T-shirt torn by some rough prole with no manners, would we, lads! Snobbery is always vile, but inter-youth snobbery always strikes me as peculiarly sad, as it implies that someone is *so* insecure that they have to use the lower social origins of others to make themselves feel more adequate/special even though they are still in possession of youth, hope and potential. This foul modern phenomenon was best illustrated to me in the summer of 2005 when I heard the Kaiser Chiefs, one of the inexplicably 'hot' bands of the moment, singing about girls 'with no clothes on' borrowing 'a pound for a condom' while being attacked by a 'man in a tracksuit' on their song 'I Predict a Riot'.

Frankly, these lyrics could have come unabridged from a shock-horror chav-Britain hate-editorial in any given *Daily Mail*. Yet this was a beat combo which claimed to be the hot-blooded guardians of the punk flame of 1977! Hardly, lads – that was John Lydon, Steven Jones and Paul Cook, *not* John Redwood, Steven Norris and Paul Johnson.

Similarly, in diversity-crazed, no-airs Brighton I have come across the most extraordinary snobbishness, often amongst people I know, and who should know better – and who, if I am forced to play snooty advocate, were hardly raised in the heady atmosphere of the top-drawer themselves. There is the gay man from a Northern working-class family who sees nothing incongruous or offensive in referring to a group of Southern working-class people as a 'chavalanche'. There was my friend, a single mother living on benefits, who derided local kids as 'townies' and habitués of Brighton's most famous estate as 'Whitehawk trash'. And in a story of snobbishness almost splendid in its audaciousness, a girl gardener I employed from a famously working-class area was working for a Labour councillor much respected for her devotion to her constituents. Imagine my gardener's surprise when she came quietly into the house in search of her honest day's pay to find the People's Friend on the phone, spieling out the most poisonous stream of invective regarding the sexual conduct, employment prospects and group IQ of the very people who had elected her! My friend, who came from that very neighbourhood, dropped her very large, very muddy garden shears on the Janus-faced joker's immaculate white carpet; when the duplicitous dunce turned with a start, my friend said quietly, 'I come from X.'

'Oh!' exclaimed the People's Friend in disbelief. 'But you've got your *own business*!'

With friends like that, who needs class enemies?

In a city where the ruling New Labour elite has shown a decidedly unhealthy interest in 'managing' the indigenous working class by means as extreme as sending them to resettle in Milton Keynes, or sticking them all in a satellite town and shipping them in to labour each day, it seems strange that there is such a whole-hearted welcome for incomers. You'd think that a local paper, which regularly ran headlines along the lines of DOOMED, DOOMED, WE'RE ALL DOOMED! whenever half a dozen maisonettes were put up or it failed to rain for three days, would think that the region was a bit, well, overcrowded and under-resourced already. But apparently our part of Sussex, like our sceptred island in general, is only too full of *indigenous* people. *They're* the reason why our hospitals are breaking down and our classrooms are overfull and unemployment is the highest it's been for a decade. But if people come here from overseas, see, they immediately *make it better*! Thus throughout 2006, the Brighton *Argus*, between bouts of hand-wringing and chest-beating over drought and over-development, saw fit to run an alternative set of rather more cheery if utterly self-contradicting headlines such as CITY IS HOME TO THE WORLD ('Influx of foreign nationals brings diverse culture') and CITY HAS BECOME PEOPLE MAGNET.

This last screamer, of 29 August 2006, recorded that B&H was recording its most rapid rise in population since the 1960s – two-thirds of incomers coming from overseas – and was now, for the first time, growing faster than the nation's capital. No need to fear, however! Even though we are book-ended by the sea and the Downs, with apparently nowhere left to build except up. And then, of course, we can expect the usual bed-wetters banging on about 'soulless' tower blocks – as if 'family houses' actually have souls! Now *that's* what I as a Christian call blasphemy, but we'll let it go, in the name of 'diversity', no doubt.

'City leaders say the rising population can bring a wealth of benefits,' crooned the *Argus*, as it stroked the collective brow of a bug-eyed readership terrified that their dinky little playpen by the sea was now bulking up even quicker than the collapsing colossus so many of us had come here fleeing from. Such benefits would include 'extra grants per head of population from the Government,' the piece stumbled gamely on, over the sound of bullets entering toes at a rate of knots. 'And it can help to fill gaps in the labour market,' the paragraph finished lamely, not to say ungrammatically.

Which left the reader feeling distinctly unconvinced – like, wow! We're the lowest paid and highest unemployed place in the whole of the South East, and we're meant to get out the bunting and throw street parties because the Government/local council is welcoming in a whole heap of *cheap labour* to make our situation even more desperate! Once again, let the white working class give thanks to their rulers for showing them the light – Gawd bless yer, Guv!

But 'After the Lord Mayor's Show comes the shit', as the Cockneys have it. And in the wake of the initial excitable cheerleading – 'Economic forecasters say the arrival of workers from abroad could boost the city's economy by as much as £10 million a year!' (love that 'could'; like beauty products which 'may' halt signs of ageing. But equally, logically speaking, could/may not) – the hard facts and creeping fears came piling up thick and fast. 'However, while councillors and MPs welcomed the boost, they have warned the Government that infrastructure such as housing, hospitals, transport, water supplies and schools must improve and grow along with the population.'

Yes – and if wishes were horses, beggars would ride. And there would be an awful lot more of the stuff that follows the Lord Mayor's Show, just as surely as the reality of an open-door immigration policy – sex slavery, child peddling, £3.3 billion in unpaid taxes from half a million illegal foreign workers (according to the latest, extremely embarrassing police report; enough to build 132 schools or 13 hospitals, apparently!) – follow the high-minded eulogies to it. It may be true that once upon a time the dream of unrestricted migration to this country had something to do with the Brotherhood of Man; these days, though, it has more to do with the Confederation of British Industry and their fellows both high and low, domestic and foreign, CEO and gangmaster, in the fetid fraternity of exploitation.

Despite this, as ever, it is the indigenous working class who are once again portrayed as the fat white flies in the joyous rainbow ointment of cultural diversity – spoiling everything for civilised people, like they did with their dirty old nets back in the day! – set up against the allegedly noble, chaste, hard-working new immigrants as the undeserving/deserving poor come back to haunt us once more. But frankly I find it both risible and offensive how quickly journalists from liberal newspapers, who in theory revere the trades union movement and the worker's struggle, so quickly become fervent supporters of free-market politics when it means they can get a dirt-cheap Croatian au pair or Polish plumber, and are so willing to swallow the reactionary old lie about how the British workforce is too idle to do certain jobs.

I'd argue, on the other hand, that when an adult human being refuses to do a job for less than £5 an hour it doesn't signal idleness at all, but simply a certain amount of dignity and self-worth, and a very understandable reluctance, after the long hard struggle of the British working class, to simply roll over and do tricks for pennies. One longs for the day when their editors decide that it really doesn't make sense to take on British hacks any more when you can get some eager, obedient, East European journalism graduate to do the job for half the price; if that day ever comes, you can bet that this Slav-sucking attitude will be out of the window quicker than you can say 'I'm all right, Jakob!' Until then, who cares about a bunch of whining proles? Racists! Even worse – CHAVS!

JORDAN: A VERY BRIGHTON SEX SYMBOL

WOMEN NOW EMPOWERED BY EVERYTHING A
WOMAN DOES

Oberlin, OH – According to a study released Monday, women – once empowered primarily via the assertion of reproductive rights or workplace equality with men – are now empowered by virtually everything the typical woman does.

'From what she eats for breakfast to the way she cleans her home, today's woman lives in a state of near-constant empowerment,' said Barbara Klein, professor of women's studies at Oberlin College and director of the study. 'As recently as 15 years ago, a woman could only feel empowered by advancing in a male-dominated work world, asserting her own sexual wants and needs, or pushing for a stronger voice in politics.'

Klein said that clothes-shopping, once considered a mundane act with few sociopolitical implications, is now a bold feminist statement. 'Shopping for shoes has emerged as a powerful means by which women assert their autonomy,' Klein said. 'Owning and wearing dozens of pairs of shoes is a compelling way for a woman to announce that she is strong and independent, and can shoe herself without the help of a man. She's saying, "Look out, male-dominated world, here comes me and my shoes." '

Whereas early feminists campaigned tirelessly for improved health care and safe, legal access to abortion, often against a backdrop of public indifference or hostility, today's feminist asserts control over her biological destiny by wearing a baby-doll T-shirt with the word 'Hoochie' spelled in glitter.

©*The Onion* 2003

I 'll lay my cards on the table here. I didn't just include the above sliver of satire from the magnificent *Onion* just to bump up my wordage – though I'd be lying if I said that wasn't a tiny part of its appeal – but because I consider it to be one of the most spot-on critiques of ill-sorted fem-prop ever written.

It's generally true that, if you're smart, when you hear some dumb cow mewling on about how empowering it is to learn pole dancing, you want to give her a good shove under the racehorse that killed Emily Wilding Davison. But then, if you're even smarter, you think: 'Hang on, chucking yourself under a racehorse is pretty dumb too – and lives up to the unjust female stereotypes of the self-sacrificing martyr and the hysteric. Sod it, pass me that thong and those tassels!'

Increasingly, I find that I am equally annoyed by uptight prisses who seem to believe that if women dress sexy, be it for pleasure or profit, they are in some way doing the dirty on everything feminism ever stood for. There are various reasons why they might think this. One is a rather pathetic lack of comprehension of how working-class women experience life. It's all very well for bourgeois bossy-boots to bleat on about women having 'worthwhile' jobs – as if being a 'journalist' was in any way 'worthwhile'! It's all about fun and fame, in my experience. But when you're given a crap education and then find that all the best jobs – even the ones that used to be available to bright working-class kids, such as, ahem, journalism – are bed-blocked by well-connected, talent-free, middle-class tossers, taking one's kit off in return for the same money in one day as you'd get keeping it on for one month starts to look not just attractive but sensible.

Accusing glamour models of being traitors to the cause, and implying that if they covered their asses up a non-sexist Eden would miraculously appear, also ignores the fact that the countries where women dress the most 'modestly' also have the least human rights: to work, to education, to choose who to have sex with. Most women would opt for a country with porn and equal rights legislation than no porn and stoning to death for adultery and the living death of the burka.

It's also too easy to see commercialised sex as a thing about men oppressing women – until you consider gay male culture. The fetishisation of fitness, youth, the body, pin-ups and porn – gay male culture has all this in spades. Does it mean that gay men hate each other? No. They are realistic about the fact that there is a tough, sleazy, strictly physical side to sex as well as a cuddly-wuddly one. At the end of the day, a nice pair of tits is a nice pair of tits and – like a nice bum on a boy – is neither the fall of Rome nor the meaning of life. And if anyone can't appreciate both, as part of a fully balanced diet, I feel sorry for them.

It is from this clearly stated position that I come to consider Jordan, the massively successful glamour model who is well on the way to becoming a sort of singularly sexy Mother Courage due to her various experiences with ill health, love rats and extreme motherhood. As luck would have it, Jordan is a Brighton born and bred girl, but I've wanted to write about her for ages anyway, always refusing at the last minute in case I went *too* far over the top attempting to defend her – as if she needs defending by a ponce like me, magnificently Tough Broad that she is! – from the monstrous legions of morons who hate her with a passion that seems completely and weirdly out of all proportion. Like, ahem, this, from Brighton's *Argus* in February 2004:

BURCHILL HAILS ICON JORDAN
Writer Julie Burchill has hailed Brighton glamour girl Jordan as a feminist icon.

Jordan, 25, is one of the favourites to win the ITV show *I'm A Celebrity . . . Get Me Out Of Here!* Almost a week into the programme, being filmed in the Australian jungle, she has infuriated John Lydon, former lead singer of the legendary Sex Pistols punk band, who called her talentless. But Hove-based Julie Burchill said: 'I love Jordan's breathtaking bluntness and lack of hypocrisy and her stoicism and complete lack of self-pity in an age when we are all encouraged to be neurotic cry-babies or to be condemned as "in denial".

'She seems to have been created by some mad feminist genius scientist. She has never made a life in the skin trade seem like a smiley, harmless romp, as Page Three girls traditionally have, but rather more like an endurance test. I have seen her a couple of times close up in the street in Brighton and when she is not pulling that ****-me face she's quite astonishingly good looking. All in all I think she is splendid.'

Ewww – *put that tongue away*! But you'll notice, in my defence, that I didn't actually use the words 'feminist' or 'icon' at all about Jordan, either singly or together. I said she was blunt, stoic, unhypocritical, good looking, splendid – OK, a hypothetical mad feminist genius scientist got in there somewhere. But come on, no one's perfect!

There has been, by women who should know better, a full-on attempt to make Jordan and her female admirers look pretty damn stupid over the past few years. And, as with the chavscum crusade, it really makes you wonder about the sanity of those who choose to expend time and effort working themselves into a lather over these particular people rather than making a stand against those really malign individuals who degrade our society with every breath they take – racists, Islamofascists, dirty Papist paedophile priests who degrade the nobility of the Christian religion. Is it because they're scared of people with the viciousness and inclination to hit back, one wonders?

To make us look daft, they always accuse her fans of calling Jordan a feminist icon, when all we probably said was that she was a level-headed and hard-working business-woman with a nice pair of knockers – hardly the same thing. But you know, thinking about it, the performances by what are widely considered to be bona fide feminist icons – i.e., stuck-up, over-educated, middle-class cows – over the past decade have been pretty damn poor, so . . . why not? The 60s and 70s were supposed to be full of Strong Female Role Models, according to popular legend, while ever since the horrid, hollow 80s – starting with the Wicked Witch of the West, Thatcher – women have become famous, or so the why-oh-whiners of the mediaocracy would have it, only by pandering to the desires of men, be this by ignoring their 'nurturing' essence and becoming free-trade warriors, or by turning themselves into living, breathing Barbie Dolls.

What a load of old bobbins! Of course, what happened in the 1980s was that women finally cottoned on that the legend of female virtue and nurturing was the most elaborate and audacious class-action con-trick ever pulled, conveniently allowing men to bag all the fun and money life had to offer for themselves, and kicked it into touch not a moment too soon. And when we look back at the allegedly feminist icons of the 1960s and 70s, what a sad shower they seem. There's Jolly Jane Fonda, complaining in her autobiography about how she would regularly indulge in sexy threesomes with beautiful women and her husband Roger Vadim, not out of any sense of rompiness – Lord forfend! – but because, as she told a suitably awed *Vogue*, 'I think it shows how deep my fear of being without a man was, that I could convince myself of things that really hurt me.'

Even weirder was Fonda's fellow thespian and pin-up (she named her daughter after her), Vanessa Redgrave, whose surname incidentally has always struck me as quite surreally suitable, serving as she did to convince many reasonable people that to be left-wing is to be a lunatic.

Then there was Redgrave's similarly confused comrade Leila Khaled, who struggled against the liberation of her own gender under the guise of fighting for the liberation of the Palestinians, who, despite the modish window-dressing, are prey to every woman-hating vice of their leaders. Ulrike Meinhof – mmm, just what the world needed just one generation after the Second World War: a shrieking German bint with a machine gun trying to overthrow democratically elected governments! Bernadette Devlin, vociferous supporter of the Irish republican movement, at the root of which stands the supremely hypocritical, rabidly gynophobic Catholic Church. Our own dear Germaine Greer, decrying sexism while posing starkers in *Suck* magazine, and then going on to claim that a quick Western nose job is as bad as the genital mutilation of millions of girls throughout the Third World. When she isn't vomiting on a roundabout while wearing a colander on her head for the benefit of *Big Brother*, that is.

Women acting as the dupes of men in pursuit of some addled idea of Heaven on earth and beyond is with us more than ever now; all those self-loathing chumps in burkas blowing their worthless selves and priceless people to pieces in order to achieve systems of government which will delight in grinding the faces of their female friends and relatives into the dirt. They may seem a world away from the free-loving likes of Redgrave and her groupie ghouls, but they are sisters under the skin in that, whatever their high-flown rhetoric, politics to them is little more than a souped-up sock-hop at which gaining approval from whatever passed as the alpha males of the time was all-important.

Jordan, contrarily, has never been interested in being popular. She saw straight to the core of a certain sort of male sexual desire and gazed back, unflinching and un-shamed. The stony stare which she brought to Page 3 – which once boasted that it picked its girls partly 'for their smiles', a claim not as silly as it sounds when you look at girls like Linda Lusardi, whose teeth were nearly as large and attractive as their tits – recalled the way young black boxers confront the camera; nowhere to run that doesn't lead to a dead-end job paying peanuts, so best to buckle down, come off the ropes fighting, take the money and run – hopefully to a place where people are not judged by the postal districts they were born in, and where surviving and thriving has more to do with individual guts and determi-nation than with who Daddy was and who Mummy knew.

Nor is Jordan the fragile child-woman sex symbol – oops! my skirt fell off! – a look attempted by so many bright, bitter young things supremely unsuited to making it in the skin trade. The best of these by a blonde mile, after all, was Saint Marilyn, who was so soft and yielding, all the way through, that even nasty old Norman Mailer gushed that sex with her would be 'easy as ice cream' before signing off with the rather repulsively twee, 'Pay your visit to Mr Dickens, for he like many another literary man is bound to adore you, fatherless child.' Franz Kline, unintentionally summing up the vileness of food porn once and for all, opined startlingly: 'She looked like if you bid her, milk and honey would flow from her.' W.J. Weatherby seemed to think he was complimenting poor insecure Norma Jean by reassuring we mere mortals that, 'there was something indefinably shy about her, an almost old-fashioned inferiority complex and fear of rejection, a wallflower streak in the beautiful woman'. Whereas, of course, these apparently endearing charms were a source of the very poisons that contributed to her ruin.

It is highly possible to imagine Jordan coming out with some of the things Marilyn actually said – 'Money, that's what it's all about'; 'People respect you because they feel you've survived hard times and endured, and although you've become famous, you haven't become phoney'; 'I could never be a kept woman or marry just for money. I like my independence too well' – and this is understandable as they were both decent, self-made, working-class women with not one iota of nepotism or parasitism between them. But it is well nigh impossible to imagine Jordan having any of those sickly epitaphs and saccharine eulogies dripped over her heavenly body, dead or alive – and a good thing too, because look how poor sainted Marilyn ended up! That's where being as easy as ice cream and spurting milk and honey and being catnip to Dickens gets you.

Whereas the look in poor sweet Marilyn's eyes forever breathes down the decades 'Hi, big boy!', Jordan's point-blank gaze eternally challenges – come and have a go, if you think you're hard enough. She is Sex Object as Slugger – she never met a man she couldn't lick, nudge nudge! –

determined not to stagger away from the arena of combat punch-drunk and down at heel. That's Jordan's money you've got in your pocket, little man, the price you pay for looking so hard and so long at the Pricey, and she wants it back, every red cent of it. And if I had a daughter, I would far rather she took Katie Price as her role model than Fonda, Redgrave or Greer. Because to change your face and body, all above board, because being beautiful is your business, is one thing; to contort your sexuality and pervert your politics to a point where you work towards a goal which will actually oppress and obliterate you as a woman speaks far more of a broken spirit and a dead soul.

But then, I'm a working-class broad with huge tits who's made lots of money and become famous in her fashion. Though no longer young and beautiful, I don't feel envious of Jordan, but rather want to stand up and cheer whenever I see her smiling. Most journalists' experience, however, is not mine, and being forever on the periphery of fame and fortune, but never achieving it, can make them bitter and twisted in all sorts of ways. I remember a particularly nasty little piece appearing on the BBC website in 2002, written by one Bob Chaundy.

The article began with the announcement that Jordan's six-week-old baby was totally blind. But the unfortunate news of the handicapped baby was simply used as a springboard from which to trounce everything Jordan is ('typical of so many in our celebrity-lauded society in being famous merely for being famous. Her prize assets go before her in all their 32F abundance'), has done and aspires to be and do. The piece was full of totally unwarranted conde-scension (just who is 'Bob Chaundy'? Not a self-made multi-millionaire, I'll wager) and rather laughable pity (ditto); name-calling and hair-pulling followed by eye-wiping and chest-beating; cod psychology ('Her brashness and undoubted business nous conceals a seemingly classic case of low personal esteem') and a final damning faint praise: 'Determination is one positive attribute, at least, that Jordan is not short of.'

So Jordan has 'one positive attribute' at least, does she? Because from where I'm sitting, pretty near everything about what Jordan has done with the various hands she has been dealt have been not just positive, but a positive lesson to those of us who may be inclined towards indolence, self-pity and pointless, immobilising self-analysis. Accentuate the positive, eliminate the negative – would that all those who waste their lives licking wounds real or imagined could get one half of her gumption and just get on with it!

Loathsome though it is, this is nevertheless one of the more moderate scoldings/lectures/maulings Katie Price has received from the gentlemen and ladies – ha! – of the press over the years. When George Galloway – sucker up to Saddam Hussein, the designer and overseer of one of the post-war world's most evil and brutal dictatorships – had the sheer molten hypocrisy to call Jodie Marsh 'evil' on *Big Brother*, you really saw where the whole Jordan-as-hate-object had led, and now at long last there is a concerted attempt on the part of the media to rein in the worst excesses of their extraordinary hate-campaigns against glamour models. But why did Jordan attract such antagonism in the first place, just for showing her T&A and getting paid for it?

There is a toxic combo of envy and hypocrisy abroad amongst journalists, when they survey the lives of working-class young women who become 'famous for being famous', that they exhibit to no other strata of society. Hacks will fawn over wife-beating footballers, drool over Hollywood drunk-drivers and regularly paw themselves into a para-sexual frenzy when praising the work of monumentally foolish fashion designers. But just let one young woman, with no help from the state or injection from the taxpayer, haul herself into a higher tax bracket, whether by using her mammaries – Jordan – mouth – Jade – or simple sweet nature – Chantelle – and she will find herself on the receiving end of the sort of foul tirade usually reserved for child-killers. She will become a symbol of a sick, selfish society; she may even be part of the buildup to the Islamist backlash, as though showing off one's tits could in any way make a bunch of mad bastards madder than they are. Here is one of India Knight's crazed rants from the *Sunday Times* in October 2006:

> The white, male former foreign secretary said the veil was a 'visible statement of separation and of difference', and that he asks women who visit his surgery to remove it. And nuns? Does he demand to see their hair, too? It's open season on Islam – Muslims are the new Jews.
>
> I am particularly irked by ancient old 'feminists' wheeling out themselves and their 30-years-out-of-date opinions to reiterate the old chestnut that Islam, by its nature, oppresses women (unlike the Bible, eh?) and that the veil compounds the blanket oppression.
>
> In their view all Muslim women are crushed because they can't wear visible lipstick or flash their thongs. Does it occur to these idiots that not necessarily everyone swoons with admiration at the fact that they have won the freedom to dress like 55-year-old slappers? That perhaps there exist large sections of our democratic society, veiled or otherwise, who have every right to their modesty, just as their detractors have every right to wear push-up bras?

Knight, amongst others, attempted to set up some untenable equivalence between dressing oneself up like a parrot's cage with the cover on, on one hand – unable to smile openly, swim or feel the sun on one's face – and flashing a bit of midriff on a Saturday night. Well, yes – except one is deluded, oppressive gynophobia, and'll give you rickets, and the other's a bit of fun. And anyone who can't see the difference might as well move to Saudi Arabia right now. That'll be the Saudi Arabia where, recently, the king, previously thought to be a 'quiet reformer' Islamist, asked newspaper editors to cease publishing pictures of women because such photos could 'lead men astray'. That's the sort of madness you end up with when you read untold power into a few dirty pictures of girls – or not even dirty, or even girls, in the case of the feudal fiefdoms of the Gulf.

You can understand it from those Saudi hard-liners but the 'sex-crazed-symptom-of-a-sick-society' soothsayers of gloom'n'doom often turn out to be non-believers, and then some. Yes, more often than not, as Knight's two-toned suck-up/put-down demonstrates, those strange types who think that the Four Horsemen of the Apocalypse should be called not Pestilence, War, Famine and Death but Pussy-Pelmet, Crop-Top, Boob-Tube and Thong are journalists. That is, the most notorious profession on earth – with the possible exceptions of politicians – for its promiscuity, drunkenness, laziness, freeloading and desire for fame and fortune. (And I say that with my hand proudly up to all of those qualities but two.)

This famously being the case, what could lead an actual *Evening Standard* journalist, with no apparent irony, to write in October 2006 of the TV show *From Ladette To Lady*: 'The greatest advantage of living at this particular stage in our civilisation is that there are previously un-dreamed of riches knocking about in the field of unre-strained slappers, binge-drinking trollops and foul-mouthed tarts'? Two thoughts came to me unbidden when I read this: pot, kettle, black and, 'Ooo, somebody isn't getting their end away much these days!'

* * *

This level of almost surreal hypocrisy seems to be every-where these days, proving that there is no honour whatso-ever among thieves, slags or drunkards. This phenomenon can be seen in the persecution of several young women simply for having fun and making big bucks while doing so, who are seen as fair game for every old has-been and never-was in town. Thus in 2006 nineteen-year-old Lindsay Lohan had to suffer the double drag of a finger-wagging letter from her father – who was, if you please, in jail at the time serving four years for drunk-driving and assault! – begging her to mend her wild ways: 'Sometimes we run, we seek to hide or just escape from the pain.' (Someone's just discovered Britney Spears' songs more than half a decade after the rest of us!) And, to add insult to infamy, the septuagenarian Jane Fonda came up for air to sniff, more in sorrow than in anger: 'I think every once in a while, a very, very young person who is burning both ends of the candle needs to have somebody say, "You know, you're going to pay the piper. You better slow down",' she told Access Hollywood Tuesday. '[Lohan's] in the magazines, so you always know what she's doing because you can just read about it in the tabloids. She parties all the time . . . And you know, she's young and she can get away with it. But, you know, it's hard after a while to party very hard and work very hard. She'll learn that.'

There is something singularly repulsive about the sight of women who've slagged around with the worst of them – and if the truth be told probably didn't actually come that much, but rather put out so copiously because they were boring company and had to find a way to get in good with the boys somehow – handing out unasked-for advice to young chicks at the peak of their party-pack beauty who are probably coming at the drop of a coke spoon. To read holier-than-thou columnists, most lividly India Knight on Kate Moss in particular, and on attractive, fun-loving young women of working-class origin generally, makes one feel almost dirty by association – like having a person show you their knickers, and realising with dull dismay that they've still got last month's period stains on them. Knight's regular verbal spasms against Moss, and most of the female columnists' attacks on good-time girls, were witch-hunts with a difference – the witches were doing the hunting.

You didn't even have to be a bitter old hack to get in on the act. There was also the sumptuous hypocrisy of Helen Mirren – *Helen Mirren!* – gratuitously demonising girls for getting their kit off in the course of doing publicity for her 2006 film *The Queen* – playing a woman of reserve and dignity obviously having gone to her head. 'A world of duty, sacrifice and honour meeting up with the Walkers crisps generation of consumer celebrity, going to Ibiza, taking your top off and staggering about boasting how many guys you shagged that night.'

Helen Mirren demonising girls for getting their kit off! It's rather akin to the Grand Wizard of the KKK accusing the BNP of being racist. It is, sadly, par for the course with ageing beauties and non-beauties alike that when – repeat after me – the nipples go north, the snout goes south, and all sorts of self-deceiving silliness gets spouted.

And so we come back to Jordan, long-time whipping-girl for all the repentant round-heels in the Western world, because she has made money and kept her head. Now, due to extreme motherhood, she is pulling through the other side as a soft-porn Mother Courage. Showbiz, of course, is nothing but a big playpen, and the much-touted traumas of the mummers, crooners and jesters within it are nothing compared with the troubles of real people, but inside its lush city limits are a number of women who do make you want to stand up and cheer, women who might be described as Strong Women if the phrase had not been rendered so risible. Instead, I think of them as Hard Women: Kylie,

Kate, Joan Collins, Barbara Windsor – and now Jordan. Diverse though these examples are, they share a brazen, blameless good humour; they never explain, never complain; they are 'troupers' who have all come to a state of showbiz grace in which they understand that female toughness is an extreme form of politeness, and of grace. In an age of psycho-babble nice-speak, the demonisation of the stiff upper lip and the deification of 'vulnerability', the Hard Woman – that is, the lucky soul whose bad experiences bounce off rather than damage – threatens the touchy-feely status quo.

In a newspaper interview with the singer Blu Cantrell, the female journalist expressed prurient concern over the 'hardness' of the self-possessed star in dealing so honestly with her porno past ('I was poor, it paid the rent') and her refusal of a huge *Playboy* offer to repeat the experience because she wanted to be known for singing rather than stripping. To be so sorted, so 'hard', was shown as a character flaw, probably indicating irreversible spiritual damage; to have been a blithering Bridget McBeal idiot, vulnerable and 'troubled', would doubtless have endeared Cantrell to her examiner. It's a topsy-turvy world, all right. Bleat, whine and endlessly pick at your spiritual scars, and you'll qualify as a Strong Woman. But smile, shrug and say, 'Onwards and upwards!' and you're a suitable case for treatment. In the past, ambitious women had to pretend to be stupid to be acceptable; now, they must pretend to be complex, traumatised 'survivors'. In the light of this sexist, miserabilist orthodoxy, surely clear-eyed, hard-hearted happiness is the most maddeningly subversive weapon a woman can wield.

And wield it Jordan does, with a smile like a scalpel and breasts like bazookas. When I look at her, I see the Final Girl, the term coined by Carol J. Clover in her book *Men, Women and Chainsaws: Gender in the Modern Horror*

Film. The Final Girl is the last person standing, who is usually a female, in horror films, particularly slasher films – *Scream*, *Halloween*, *Nightmare on Elm Street*. Like Jordan, the Final Girl often has a unisex name; unlike Jordan, she is usually virginal or at least virtuous. But thinking about it, Jordan has actively won back her virtue through her most recent experience as mater dolorosa; a type of virtue based on patience and endurance which is far more precious and admirable than the few centimetres of skanky skin which our Muslim brothers define as 'honour', and honour worth killing their sisters over come to that. Yes, to my mind Jordan *is* the Final Girl of Girls – and she's not planning on going down any time soon, thank you!

We've considered Katie Price as whipping-girl, icon of class hatred, folk-demon and slasher-film heroine, but just why exactly is she – ahem – A Very Brighton Sex Symbol, pray? Well, at the risk of clutching at straws, I'd say that her ability to split herself physically into two people – Jordan falling out of basques and bars all over London, Katie riding her beloved horses across the fields of Sussex which surround her hometown – is a safeguard other glamour girls have not had. Like her grandmother, who was a topless mermaid on Hastings pier, performing behind two sheets of glass containing water and bubbles, and sacked for smoking 'underwater', she epitomises a very practical, seaside sex-iness that is a world away from, say, poor posh Sophie Anderton undergoing a tormented meltdown in the paparazzi-crazed crucible of the capital.

There are lots of people attempting to jump on the Jordan cheer-leading bandwagon who, just a couple of years ago, saw her as a symbol of all that is rotten about Western civilisation; well, I happen to think that Western civilisation knocks the crap out of any other system, so I've always liked Jordan. And you know what, I don't want to follow the herd now and start liking her for all the upright, uptight PC reasons – that she's a devoted mother, a faithful wife, a hard worker.

No – I like her because she's shameless, in the best possible way. That is, unlike a lot of people – respectable, educated and/or pious people – she has nothing to be ashamed of. The more she takes off, the more decent she becomes; even posing in *Playboy* she looks so much less conventionally trampy than the all-American Cherry Pies and Cotton Candies. Because of her true grit, and because of the overwhelming sense, in the way she looks at the camera – not flirting with it, but staring it down – of the real savvy and substance beneath the sleek, silky exterior. Even porned up to the nines there is something unnervingly classy about her. Brighton's like that; it has real depth and soul, which is why it can afford to seem trashy and fun.

And that's why Jordan is such a very Brighton sex symbol.

SKYLINE OF SHAME: THE RESPECTABLE THRILL OF OVER-REACTING TO ARCHITECTURE

O n 5 October 2006, the council met for what the local *Argus* cool-headedly described as 'the most important vote made by Brighton and Hove councillors for a generation'. They were deciding whether to approve plans for a new sports centre and housing development on the site of the King Alfred Leisure Complex, a perilously elderly sports centre-cum-derelict amusement arcade on Hove seafront. The King Alfred's main building resembled nothing so much as a scaled-down Victorian gasworks, and had been showing its age for longer than even Norman Wisdom would care to remember. They'd spruced it up in the mid-1980s with a remodelled pool and the addition of some colourful water chutes which sprouted appealingly from one of its exterior walls, but the chutes were closed owing to safety fears a few years later and left to rust; by October 2006, they looked like they'd have been more at home growing out of someone's armpit in an H.R. Giger painting.

The proposed alternative? An enlarged, £48 m sports centre

with three pools (two of which would have *moveable floors!*),[1] badminton courts, sports hall, gym, spa, crèche, etc., etc. – *plus* 751 new homes, 276 of which would be used for subsidised social housing, in a bright, modern apartment complex with its own shops, restaurants, police station and doctor's surgery. And all of this would be built to the specifications of renowned architect Frank Gehry, a man whose work routinely draws the attention of the whole world to any two-bit, one-horse town he deigns to set it down in.

Not much of a toughie, you might think – especially if you considered how many years it had taken for the Gehry plan to reach such an advanced stage, and how many more it would undoubtedly take for any alternative proposal to get as far. We needed new homes and a new sports centre, so why not just go ahead and build them? Ah, but it wasn't as simple as that. What if they looked a bit weird?

Such was the central plank of opposition to the proposal, which came from all the expected sources (the Brighton Society, the *Argus* letters page, anyone with an interest in sailing or water-colours) as well as from an entirely new pressure group created especially for the occasion: 'saveHOVE'. In fairness, Gehry's plan clearly *was* a bit weird in a whole number of ways, chief among them being that the twin towers at its centre were to be festooned with curved glass sails, to create the illusion of rippling movement. The architect said this feature had been inspired by the long, flouncy dresses he'd seen women wearing in pictures of Edwardian Brighton, and that the five-building complex as a whole was designed to create the impression of 'five beautiful women, five madonnas'. Predictably, the good people of saveHOVE knew better. As they explained on their website:

> The Frank Gehry designs ... are a celebration of the breakdown of society, of manic and chaotic values. It [*sic*] is

---

[1] Actually, this will probably turn out to be less exciting than it sounds.

loud, brash, harsh, aggressive, violent. The architectural equivalent of the nihilistic punk values of the 1970's (and today's Rap) fused with the regimented brutalist functional-ism of an earlier part of the 20th Century. Visual anarchy. Thrash-metal music in a serene setting. An expression of open contempt for Hove's entire present reality: its tree-lined avenues, listed buildings, classic squares, conservation areas, quiet dignity and values. Shockitecture.[2]

So they're like punk, rap and thrash metal . . . *all at the same time*? Regimented *and* anarchic? Talk about a fusion of disparate elements – this Gehry feller must be even more of a genius than they say! That's the funniest thing about objections like this: they end up giving modern architecture far more credit for 'represen-ting' stuff than even its staunchest and most pretentious advocates would ever dare. Despite its trendy abuse of the laws of capitalisation, saveHOVE was clearly an organisation at odds with the modern world per se, which it semi-coherently defined in terms of 'constant light, traffic noise and pollution, enervating drug or caffeine-driven, aggressive and challenging hyperactivity, all-night drinking, tension, fashionable competition and new, new, **newer**'. In opposing the Gehry development, its members had at last found a sturdy peg on which to hang all that glowering disapproval, and hang it they damned well would – even if that meant ascribing near-Godlike powers of artistic alchemy to the unwitting Mr Gehry.

Sitting at the other, less hysterical end of the conservationist spectrum is the Brighton Society, whose fusty-but-fair approach has earned it such widespread respect that even the council occasionally defers to its judgement. Sadly, however, it too found itself unable to resist the lure of folly while fulminating over the Gehry plans, referring to the lower-rise buildings surrounding the

---

[2] Hey, is that a *pun*? Even though 'Shock' sounds nothing like 'Arch' and all the letters are different? *Well done you!*

towers as 'Soviet style'. Although, admittedly, I haven't been to Russia since the late 1980s, the nearest thing I ever saw to one of those buildings was actually part of 'Atlantis', an American-run theme hotel in the Bahamas; even with the Cold War long gone, are we seriously to believe that American property developers have started apeing the styles of classical Russian architecture? It seems rather more likely that the Society's correspondent in this instance was, well, 'getting on a bit', with an imagination that hadn't worked hard enough to generate anything like fear since they last read a John le Carré novel some time in 1983. Consequently, whenever anything comes along that looks even the least bit threatening or unpredictable: *Hmmm ... Looks a bit Russian to me ...*

In both these cases, however, the real problem is not necessarily that the campaigners concerned are too old and/or square to embrace change but simply that *they take architecture too personally.* So there's a building you don't much like the look of down the road – so what? It'll annoy you every time you pass by for about six months and then you'll stop noticing it, because that's the way our perceptual equipment works. Does it have to *say* something about you? Do you have any right or reason to feel ashamed *or* proud of it, given that you had absolutely nothing to do with putting it there? Might your time not be better employed if you just tried worrying about something else?

A saveHOVE stalwart would no doubt reply that the King Alfred development was worth fighting in case it proved to be the thin end of a wedge; if we'd let this one pass, the logic goes, we'd all have woken up one morning ten years later to find ourselves living in 'high-rise hell'. This might well be a reasonable argument when applied to a younger, less established town, but as far as Brighton or Hove go, it's plainly absurd. Yes we *do* have a high proportion of beautiful old buildings, but we'll still have every one of them in ten years' time because *there's a law that says you can't pull them down.* As for what happens to the rest, I'm not terrifically bothered – most of them don't have anything in particular to recommend them. And if an old, low-rise but criminally ugly building (like, oh I don't know … the King Alfred Leisure Complex?) were to be demolished to make way for a brand new skyscraper which actually looks kind of cool, I for one would not be churlish enough to grizzle about it.

I almost was, though. When I first saw a scale model of the Gehry development at the Jubilee Library I was as shocked as anyone – so much so that, when they asked me to record my opinion on a little slip of paper, I simply fled. Even then I knew I quite liked the cut of its jib, but it just looked so outlandish that I couldn't help thinking, as many a saveHOVE activist before me had thought, 'It's wrong for Hove.' In the months that followed, however, its picture appeared in our local rags (all the free ones – and that other one) numerous times, and every time I saw it I felt just a little bit keener. There's something quite exciting about the prospect of having such an exotic beast on one's own doorstep; it wouldn't make me feel *proud*, exactly, but it's always encouraging to see a flagrantly eccentric plan actually come to fruition because it proves that the world can be less predictable than we sometimes like to think. Anything as flat-out *bizarre* as Gehry's design carries with it a sense of limitless possibility, of absolute freedom – and if that's what the future's going to be about then for flip's sake let's just get on with it.

As for it being 'wrong for Hove', well, it might pay to recall a certain historical precedent. When the Pavilion first went up it appalled practically everyone in Brighton, but when it was threatened with demolition a little less than thirty years later they voted in favour of using public money to buy it. Many still loathed it – the motion was only carried by 1,343 votes to 1,307 – but it was clearly starting to win people over. Nowadays, of course, the idea of touching so much as one freaky minaret on its head seems almost monstrous, even to those who still insist on calling it 'tacky', because it's impossible to imagine Brighton without it. To the rest of the world it has become the recognised shorthand for *us* – hence its appearance on the front cover of this very book – and none of this would have happened had it not, in the first place, been so obviously 'inappropriate'. No one ever tried to build anything that inappropriate around here again until Gehry came along, so we have no empirical means of knowing whether or not it's possible to repeat the trick. But wouldn't it be fun to try?

Having said all that, aesthetic rectitude was actually the less significant of the campaigners' two principal concerns; more than anything else they were just childishly overexcited about all the new friends they were about to make. 'Hove,' saveHOVE thundered, 'is under siege. We are looking at hugely increased numbers of people living here.' This was, to some extent, true – inevitably so, given the recent surge of interest in Brighton and the fact that every council in the country was trying to meet government-set targets for building new homes – but there wasn't a lot we could do about it, short of declaring Hove an independent republic. Nor was there much anyone could do about the fact that the only brownfield site (mmm – lovely image) suitable for the kind of large-scale development Hove needed was the King Alfred. It wasn't just suitable, it was almost ideal: spectacular sea views, handy for the shops, and if the newcomers turned out to be noise polluters they'd only be bothering neighbours on one side.

Oh, but the *shops*! It may actually have been quite insensitive of me to even mention them, because this was yet another thing the nay-sayers seemed determined to panic about. Brian Oxley, one of several Conservative councillors who opposed the scheme,[3] was quoted as saying it would be 'like a small village . . . the seafront cannot sustain that sort of development. No extra shops or schools are being proposed.' About schools I freely admit I know nothing whatsoever, but I can say for certain that there are loads of shops around there already; they're just easy to overlook because so many of them are either very boring or very

---

[3] What is it with the Tories these days? Do they not believe in 'letting the market decide' any more? They'll be on at us to reopen the coal mines next.

boarded up. It doesn't take a *huge* leap of the imagination to visualise the still-functioning ones losing that moribund, half-day-closing ambience and stocking up on things people actually want to buy, or selling up for an extortionate sum to someone who will. A few of those old places – like 'Dresswell's of Hove' or time-warp tobacconist E. Burkitt Ltd – are gems it would be a tragedy to lose, but for this very reason they might stand a better chance of prospering were a large influx of kitsch-loving Londoners to be placed in their vicinity. I won't deny that the thought of our noble shopkeepers being condescended to by those barbarians tends to set my teeth on edge but, you know, needs must.

Even leaving that aside, who's to say how many shops any given number of people will need? Some people shop more than others! The sad fact is, someone or other will *always* come out with that 'overstretched resources' jive *whenever* there seems an increased risk of a few more people being around. Only the starriest-eyed of humanists could fail to quail at the thought of their own cosy backwater being suddenly inundated by hordes of strangers with unknown intentions, and no one who wasn't literally a zombie would be untouched by peevishness upon learning that they were going to be living next door to a building site for many months if not years. Both of these are perfectly natural reactions; the weird thing is, people who protest against low-impact urban renewal[4] very seldom mention having had them. You *know* they have, because it's the only possible explanation for all the emotional language they use, but they'll never just come out and say so because they (rightly) fear the disgrace of being branded a 'Nimby'. And maybe, at the backs of their minds, they realise that these *honest* objections are rhetorically counter-productive, because any rational person will simply

---

[4] Just to clarify, I'm only talking about the kind that involves pulling down worthless buildings and putting up useful ones. When it comes to pulling down anything half-decent, destroying areas of natural beauty, etc., I can get pretty shirty myself!

reply, 'People have got to live somewhere' or, just possibly, 'Pull yourself together.' This, in turn, makes them feel obliged to dress up their emotional disquiet as something more thoughtful, and they subsequently end up opposing new housing developments for all *sorts* of mad 'reasons' (as we have seen).

It is to their credit, in a way, that so many of them fail to pull off the deception convincingly. Here's Valerie Paynter of saveHOVE, talking to the *Argus* about the council's attitude towards the Gehry project: 'It's almost like they've accepted the Benidorming of the seafront.' These comments were echoed by an anonymous fellow fulminator on the saveHOVE website: 'Our seafront is in peril. Those wanting us to become another Benidorm must be stopped.' The last time I heard anyone refer to Benidorm as though it *represented* something was probably the wrong side of 1989 but it had, throughout that decade, been a regular visitor to half-arsed sitcom scripts and *Guardian* readers' nightmares alike. For the scriptwriters this was partly because, like 'Slartibartfast' in *The Hitch-Hiker's Guide to the Galaxy*, it sounded like a rude word without actually being one. But they also shared the *Guardian* readers' conviction that the Spanish resort was an over-developed hell-hole, full of drunken, bellowing proles pissing away the precious holiday time they could have spent exploring local ruins on an endless conga line of unspeakable vulgarity.

It strikes me that the world is actually not at all short of ridiculously over-developed towns and cities, any one of which these people could have used to illustrate their point. Why, then, did they go straight for Benidorm – not once but twice? Do their remarks perhaps betray a distrust not only of high-rise buildings but also of the kind of people who traditionally occupy them? Two hundred and seventy-six out of 751 units is a whole lot of social housing, particularly in the context of an area where 'social' just means a sort of office party. No wonder saveHOVE felt that Hove was 'under siege' – a phrase which literally refers to *an invasion by a hostile power* – for what could such people possibly find to enjoy in a peaceful idyll like Hove but robbery, violence and indiscriminate puking?

Happily, there was less cause for concern than they might have feared. For one thing, most of the social housing units in the Gehry plan were actually earmarked for key workers – those funny little people who prop up our infrastructure. And with good reason: as Roger French, managing director of the Brighton Bus and Coach Company, told the *Argus*, 'We are continually finding that our key workers, cleaners and drivers, are having to travel further and further away. It's a complete travesty that this development could be in jeopardy.' Nurses, teachers and fire-men's representatives in Brighton had all made similar comments over the previous few years; it was a very bad 'place to be' indeed for anyone interested in making themselves useful.

Providing affordable housing for the people it most depends upon should, by rights, be one of any city's most important responsibilities, but it seemed our municipal overlords had overlooked that small detail somewhere in the course of their rush for city status. Now they were trying to redress the balance and, for once, they deserved all our support; whingeing about overstretched resources was not an option because what *are* 'key workers' if not a kind of resource? (The only thing worse than an overstretched resource is a resource you can't even use because (s)he's got snowed in at Hurstpierpoint.) If you're happy to let them drive you around or set your arm in plaster, you should be happy to have them live next door to you. Even if they talk or dress too loudly or in ways you cannot understand, take heart: it's a scientific fact that, at the end of a long day, over 99 per cent of them will simply be too exhausted to throw an irate Rottweiler through your picture window.

It could all have been so very different if only a few more of them had been *Hove* key workers instead of Brighton ones. saveHOVE's rhetoric flirted heavily with the implication that, with the King Alfred development, Hove was being made to pay for Brighton's innumerable sins – specifically the 'aggressive and challenging hyperactivity' that had driven it to expand so recklessly. Snobbery about Brighton was, of course, nothing new to Hove: it had been a running joke amongst Brightonians for decades that Hove was really called 'Hove Actually', because whenever some impertinent pup asked a resident of Hove whether they lived in Brighton, that was how they invariably replied. The weird, neurotic, impotently raging brand of snobbery that sometimes came to the fore during the King Alfred debate, however, *was* quite a new thing, and it was motivated by some very specific political factors. Take it away, saveHOVE . . .!

> Following the creation of the unitary authority which strip-ped Hove of its autonomy as a self-governing town there has been a fairly obvious and clench-jawed campaign to put Hove in its place as Brighton's subservient 'other half'. One of saveHOVE's number describes Hove as 'Brighton's battered wife'.

So *that's* what it was all about – they were just paranoid that they hadn't being getting proper representation since the amalgamation of Brighton and Hove's councils! In this case, I can honestly sympathise. An amalgamated council was *always* going to pay more attention to Brighton's interests than Hove's, if only because it's bigger, wealthier and more fun to rule; *that's yet one more reason why the whole amalgamation/city status idea was fundamentally flawed.* Then again, Hove presumably still had the same number of councillors as before – so where had *they* been in all of this? Perhaps, dazzled by the big city lights, they'd all got their noses pierced and disappeared into Brighton's twilit underworld. But whatever the reasons for their seeming inaction, they were clearly the ones responsible for it; blaming Brighton alone for the King Alfred development was passive-aggressive thinking of the most deluded kind.

Nor did the claim that Hove had become 'Brighton's battered wife' hold much water when you took into account the fact that, *at the very same time* a short distance down the road in Brighton's fashionable Kemp Town, scores of residents were getting up in arms about a very similar development at the Marina. Similar, but slightly different: they were looking at 900 units compared to Hove's measly 751 and at least nine years' building time to its five, not to mention the fact that there were also plans to build a 12,000-seat arena on a neighbouring site (Black Rock). They also had significantly better grounds for objection than the Hove protestors, because the design for *their* proposed development directly contravened the Brighton Marina Act of 1968, which specified that nothing in the Marina could be built higher than the cliffs behind it. Needless to say, Kemp Town's campaigners had also made liberal use of the 'overstretched resources' argument, but in their case it seemed rather more justified. It was literally impossible to imagine how 12,000 people could either enter or leave the Black Rock site by car in under five hours; the main seafront road they'd all have to use gets pretty busy even outside peak times. Not only did the council have no plans to widen this road or supplement it with new ones, they would have been quite unable to do so because there were so many listed buildings in the way.

If Hove truly was 'Brighton's battered wife', then, it was surely married to the most compulsive and ostentatious self-harmer in history. What the Marina plan appeared to demonstrate was that we really are all in this together; no town or city can remain completely static, and now more than ever anyone who lives in one must face the fact that there *will* be new buildings occasionally. If those buildings seem genuinely ugly or impractical to you then by all means protest away – but complaining that they are 'inappropriate' by dint of being too modern, large or flat-out bizarre is itself no longer appropriate. Nothing beautiful or useful can ever be truly inappropriate, just as nothing ugly or redundant can ever fail to be.

The trouble with this, of course, is that there will never be a public consensus about what is and isn't 'beautiful'. But in Brighton, at least, there are encouraging signs that the overwhelming majority of residents *can* agree about such things. When plans were first drawn up to build the 'i360' – a 600-foot spire with a doughnut shaped 'pod' travelling up and down it to afford visitors a 25-mile view of Brighton, Hove and the surrounding countryside – the sheer boldness of the design, coupled with the fact that they were proposing to build it right where the entrance to the West Pier used to be, made a bitter and protracted debate seem almost inevitable. This failed to materialise, though; we heard the odd muffled bleat from residents of neighbouring Regency Square, but the Brighton Society et al. had very little to say about it. Even the West Pier Trust was on side, with Professor Fred Gray (a director of the Trust and an expert on seaside architecture to boot) declaring, 'I think it is fantastic. I'd love to go up there.' Me too! And it would just be *so nice* to think that this spirit of level-headed compromise could be carried forward into the debate about whatever the next eyesore/exciting modern development turns out to be – because there is no doubt in my mind that when we're all up in that pod, glancing at the completed Gehry complex on one side before turning to observe the Marina Towers on the other, it'll be hard to remember what all the fuss was about. They'll just be . . . buildings.

But what of that generation-defining council vote – how did it turn out? Well, they voted in favour of the Gehry development by nine votes to six; it then transpired that the plans would also have to be approved by a planning application sub-committee which, because of a backlog, would be unable to consider them until some time in 2007. Get ready for the most important vote *in living memory* . . .

THE COUNCIL'S NEW CLOTHES

As a precocious teen I dreamed of being Graham Greene. Well, as it turned out, I never wrote a great novel, sadly, and I never converted to Catholicism, happily, but I did do one thing he did. That is, in middle age I moved to a seaside town and got into a right barney with the local powers-that-be. Yeah, I *know*!

Even here, of course, G.G. did it with considerably more glamour, bravery and sheer molten drama than I. He moved to Antibes in 1966, and in 1982 published *J'Accuse – The Dark Side Of Nice*, in which he claimed that organised crime flourished in the shimmering suntrap, and that upper levels of the local government had protected and were protecting copious numbers of corrupt judges and police. This led to a viciously fought libel case, which the great man lost – only to be vindicated three years after his death when the former mayor of Nice was convicted of numerous counts of corruption and associated crimes and sent to jail. So basically, he fought government, gangsters, police and judges, all at once; lost – and STILL won!

I, on the other hand, moved to Brighton, then Hove, in 1995 and spent the next ten years squabbling with the local

New Labour council. Yes, I *said* I know! But 'from each according to his abilities' and all that.

So what did we squabble about? Here, for your leisurely perusal, are a few examples.

RUBBISH, LACK OF COLLECTION OF

I know that Brighton is famously a mixture of the seedy and the elegant, but in the summer of 2001 seediness swamped elegance hands down. As the sun set over the country's newest city, the stench from uncollected rubbish seemed to offer itself up like a particularly cheap and irresistible metaphor.

Once, this went on for three weeks. It was a privatisation thing; SITA, they were called, an exotically starletish name masking a mundane balls-up of an outfit. Because privatisation puts wringing every last drop of profit before anything else, SITA were forever messing with the schedule, changing routes and sacking bin-men; naturally the bin-men didn't go too much for this, and eventually went on strike, though they did very sweetly offer to work for nothing and clear the rubbish on a voluntary basis when it piled up too much. But the council said no, in case it upset SITA.

SITA in Sussex – like Railtrack nationally at the time, who were forever throwing hissy fits and blubbing when accused of poncing off the taxpayer – seemed to get upset quite easily, though maybe it would have been more appropriate for the local taxpayer to feel this way. SITA were a French company being paid £6.7 million a year by the council to keep the streets clean, and somehow managing to fail dismally at this while making losses of around £250,000 a week – or were until they threw in the towel in the aforesaid summer of 2001. But still the rubbish lay uncollected in the streets, as the council – determined to throw good money after bad – searched for yet another private refuse collecting corporation to throw cash at.

But we shouldn't have been looking at the rubbish festering in the gutter, should we! No, we should have had our eyes fixed on the stars. Or rather on the council's latest gimmick – the search for nine residents who 'want to change their lives over nine weeks – whether it's by getting fit or using the car less, sorting out their finances, saving energy or recycling more'. Said the council leader, Ken Bodfish, 'In true TV makeover fashion, we have drafted in a team of experts, from financial advisors to top chefs, personal trainers to organic gardeners, to guide the volunteers through the highs and lows of their own personal challenges.' The lucky nine were given camcorders with which to make video diaries of their personal 'journeys'. The purpose of the whole fandango was allegedly to get across the message of 'Sustainability – ensuring a better quality of life for everyone, now and for generations to come.' As opposed to being wiped out by a twenty-first-century plague spread by super-rats grown robust on a month's uncollected garbage, one presumes!

B&H council has always been the Model Village equiv of the New Labour government; spending hundreds of thousands of pounds on the city bid as the schools and hospitals here slid into dreadful disrepair was typical of its all-fur-coat-and-no-knickers aspirations. But this particular abomination, as the fetid waste lay rotting in the street, really said it all. Not that it's just we on Silly Silicone Beach who suffer from a dementedly media-obsessed local government, or that it's anything new; 'B.P.' wrote me a savagely amusing letter recalling the time in the late 1970s when she worked with a voluntary organisation attempting to cushion the extreme poverty of some King's Cross residents. Hearing of their plight, the Greater London Arts Authority – rolling in it, as per – sent a representative down to the 'Cross to address a meeting of local women from council estates.

They listened attentively to her lecture on what the GLAA was about and how the community could be revived through the arts and so on. And then they said that all they wanted was some money to start a dressmaking group to make clothes for themselves and their children; they wondered whether the GLAA could help with a few hundred pounds for some sewing machines. X exploded and said that she was 'not in the business of setting up sewing circles' – but if they wanted money for camcorders or setting up a street theatre group, she would be delighted to help. They politely told her to get stuffed and got on with their own fund-raising; the GLAA money went, of course, to all the trendy middle-class wankers who were flocking to such an up-and-coming area, most of whom have now sunk happily into the bosom of New Labour. Sad, isn't it?

Sad – but true. All the people of this country – and probably any other come to that – want from government, via their taxes, are decent public services: schools, hospitals and transport; this is the covenant which has served us well, in our modest way, since the end of the War. But even as taxes continue to rise, a lower proportion goes on these essentials than ever before. Instead it goes on bailing out the private companies who screw up our utilities and on unutterably lame 'initiatives'. Where are Drug Czar Keith Halliwell and Homelessness Czarina Louise Casey now, one wonders? Government by Gameshow, you could call it; the rubbish lies uncollected and the trains won't work when the weather is 'wrong', but look on the bright side: you can always divert yourself from your troubles by clowning around with a council-lent camcorder for a few weeks.

The real high rollers, of course, get the big prizes; transport, hospitals, schools. Really, what is it with New

Labour and privatisation? Even Mrs Thatcher wouldn't touch the Post Office and the railways, let alone start dicking around with the prison system. And at least in her case, privatisation was about ideology and therefore understandable if misguided. With Labour, getting rid of public utilities – or in the case of local Labour councils, farming out contracts to private companies – seems to be some sort of bizarre obsessive-compulsive disorder – 'Eww, trains – dirty!' – like with those weird women who have one thing surgically altered and then can't stop till everything's been renovated. If this country looked like a person right now, it would probably look a lot like Michael Jackson; a perfectly decent specimen to start with which for some reason convinced itself that it would look a lot better with everything taken off and put back on inside out and upside down.

It works both ways; half the country couldn't be bothered to vote because the election was like a really dull gameshow when you know who's going to win and don't like any of them anyway. And that being so, gimmicky initiatives are the last thing that will win them over. It's a bit of a joke that politicians are meant to be the serious-minded grown-ups and the electorate the frivolous thrill-seeking types, but voters have never, to my knowledge, *expressed* an actual desire for prizes and makeovers among the political options offered to them. No, all we generally want is to have our loved ones educated decently when young, treated decently when sick and old and to be able to get from London to Manchester in slightly less time and for marginally less money than it takes to get from Montreal to London. As 'G.C.' put it in a letter to me, 'Historians, when they come to write about New Labour, need look no further than our council to see where it all went wrong; an administration which consistently ignores core services in order to spend its money on headline-grabbing projects which benefit an elite few.'

And if we want a lifestyle overhaul, we can cut out the middle man and call up Carol Smillie ourselves.

MONEY, TAKING FROM THE POOR AND GIVING TO THE PONCEY

Q. How can you tell Robin Hood wasn't on Brighton & Hove Council?

A. Because he didn't take from the poor and give to a mime troupe.

From the day the first middle-class ponce and/or nonce decided that he was a 'socialist', Lord help us, there's been a lot of old eyewash talked about socialism's duty to 'culture'. Ooo, let's have 'bread and circuses', let's have 'bread and roses' – let's have a poxing 'revolution for fun'. In the refreshingly non-noncey or poncey words of old man Royle – my arse!

I don't speak here as any sort of culture-hating Puritan. I regularly cry in art galleries (religious depictions of stoic suffering and full-on, bomb-Berlin-to-bits wartime propaganda do it every time for me, I find – nothing like having a broad canvas) and have even been known to go to the theatre without sneaking out at the intermission. But I will never understand how anyone who claims to be human can also claim that culture is as important as the basic human requirements of housing, healthcare and education. The money I pay for my cultural experiences came willingly from my own pocket – they were not the result of bread being removed from the mouths of the poor so that Miss Thing here could mince off to the circus smelling of roses. Which increasingly in this country, and certainly in Brighton & Hove, has been happening – ever since the Millennium Dome sprung up beside the Thames and cast its squat, shabby shadow over the new century, a monument to the callousness and corruption of politicians, and of their contempt for those who pay their wages. At a time when the previously quite rightly reviled duo 'Pimp'n'Ho' were becoming as commonplace as Sweet'n'Low or Paul and Joe, it increasingly felt, as the twenty-first century got shakily to its feet and gazed around it, that this would be the pattern of things, that the powerful pimps would send the powerless 'hos out to work in soul-destroying, exploitative jobs, then relieve them of their money in order to fritter it away on useless, self-regarding bling which served no other purpose than to make fellow pimps in the 'hood – Brussels – tell you that you da man. We were, in fact, being 'turned out' something rotten on a daily basis by the playas in the Mother of Parliaments; when the money-drenched sex lives of studs as unlikely as David Blunkett and John Prescott came to the fore, it seemed somehow appropriate. In the shadow of the Dome, how could virtue – public or private – ever flourish?

The Dome was without doubt the Daddy of all useless pimp-wear, finally swallowing more than £750 million of public money. It was estimated that this money could have paid for the following:

A hospital bed for everyone who needs one OR four new state-of-the-art hospitals

The tuition fees of a quarter of a million students over three years

A home for every homeless person

An increase of £350 a year in pensions for a decade

But what matters such humdrum drear, when Big Daddy Mack Mandelson wants something big and shiny to wear to the Sick Soul Of Europe Ball! The 'hood rats of local government worked hard to be as flash with the cash as the major ballers in Westminster, and in their provincial way they pimped their taxpayers good and hard. In 2005 there was an outcry when it transpired that East Lancashire Hospitals NHS Trust intended to spend £1 million on art, which, amazingly, they claimed would aid patients' recovery. This, despite the looming presence of a £4 million debt, which threatened to impact on actual health care! As a local MP, Nigel Evans, said, 'You don't stop to see a nice statue when you're being rushed into A&E.'

Here in Brighton and Hove over the past few years, when the council has not been busy attempting to shut down day-centres for autistic children or kick confused senior citizens out of retirement homes they imagined they'd be let alone to spend the rest of their days in, it's been throwing a huge amount of its £2 million plus discretionary grants budget at commercially driven arts organisations. In 2002, for example, it was decreed that the Brighton Festival would from then on get an annual grant in excess of £270,000 – while the Brighton Rape Crisis Project had its measly £7,000 completely axed; the only such service in Sussex, it had given comfort to thousands of victims for nearly twenty years. Said a worker for the RCS at the time, 'We are shocked that in a city which has a reputation for protecting minority rights and services for vulnerable groups, the council has diverted funds from small charities to high-profile media and arts organisations which are able to generate money themselves.' She wasn't the only one. Brighton Women's Centre were shocked, to say the least, to find that their modest annual funding had been slashed from £6,000 to a big fat zero. And this at a time when the council could pocket £2 million in parking fines over a six-month period without breaking sweat.

The people of B&H were quick to respond to this shocking show of stinginess. A subsequent council report, costing £40,000 – enough to keep the Rape Crisis Project going for more than five years – brought it the unwelcome news that the number of its citizens who believed the council did a good job had fallen from 74 to 41 per cent over two years, while those who considered it efficient and well-run had halved to just 32 per cent. To the question 'Do you think the council has sensible policies?' only 36 per cent – down from 62 – said yes.

Truly, B&H seemed to be a town without pity where its council was concerned.

CITY STATUS, CHASING OF

When I moved to Brighton from London in 1995 I was struck immediately by what I thought of as its *townliness*. A town, it seemed to me, was that perfect place to live, neither city nor country, both of which like to think they are light years apart from each other but actually have a great deal in common. That is, generally speaking, ill-temper, bad manners and the wrong number of people for the space in question – too many in the case of the city, and too few in the case of the country.

One of the worst things about London, I'd come to think, was the way that any social engagement in another postal zone needed such massive preparation, strategy and time; I'd sat in one too many taxis travelling from Bloomsbury to Brixton feeling the very will to live seep slowly away as we crawled along with all the va-va-voom of a crippled sloth on his way to the dentist, let alone the will to party-party-party-till-the-break-of-dawn! It was so far away from the turbo-charged vision of London I'd had as an impression-able provincial virgin that I could have wept; finding out that London was *sooo slooow* was far more shocking to me than finding out that there was no Santa Claus or Easter Bunny. In fact, it was on a par with finding out that Santa Claus was giving it to the Easter Bunny three different ways, on a regular basis.

But Brighton is different. Say – hypothetically, mind! – that your drug-buddy calls you up and says, 'I've scored.' Now he may be on one side of Brighton and you may be on the other, but there's every chance you'll get there before the first gram's even half gone. This, I can't help but feel, must contribute even just a little to why Brighton folk rate highest in the land for feelings of luckiness, optimism, positivity and life satisfaction, as the National Lottery survey claimed in the summer of 2006.

That we still score so high in happiness is a tribute to both the wonder of this place and the patience of its people, because for the past decade, local government has been fiddling with, niggling at and interfering in Sugartown's well-being with alarming obsessiveness, blowing oceans of local taxation into the bargain. It's almost as if the council has taken my personal motto – 'If it ain't broke, break it!' – for their municipal use. First came the merging of Brighton and Hove in 1997. As my stern collaborator points out in his opening sortie, just how plain *silly* does it sound to claim that one lives in Brighton *and* Hove, as we're meant to? Then, in the year 2000, £100,000 of our money was blown successfully chasing city status; flushed with success, 2002 saw it chasing the European City of Culture title, to the tune of another £150,000. During the course of this fool's gold rush, we awoke one morning to find that several churches had been pierced. Yes, you read that right – pierced – with huge metal rings resembling a camp King Kong's earrings. What in the world such silliness had to do with culture was anyone's guess; it didn't even display bravery or outrage, as piercing a few mosques, say, would have done. When the title finally went to Liverpool, you couldn't help but laugh – albeit hollowly, recalling that lost-and-gone-forever one hundred and fifty grand.

So what was all the endless narcissistic tinkering about, when the people of this sleazy seaside paradise seemed perfectly happy as they were? 'It's about how we're seen by the outside world,' said a council spokesman at the time. But really, who cared? Surely one of Brighton's excellent, timeless qualities has always been its what-the-hell, let-the-neighbours-buy-the-curtains recklessness. More to the point, in my opinion, was Big Minnow Syndrome.

As well as acting as a magnet to many London luminaries who have undeniably made a success of their chosen racket, B&H also attracts a number of highly ambitious types who never quite cut the Colman's in the capital and came down here not for the gorgeous sunsets or the easy living but because they can live easier with being a big fish in a small pond than vice versa. But they still feel the sting of not having made it in the big city – so they try to turn the place they're living *into* a big city.

A city! We've been a city for six years now and it *still* feels weird saying it. Can you walk across a city in half an hour? Is a city less than an hour from London, and does half its population need to go to London each morning to earn a living? Does a city have the lowest wages in the South East – lower than *Crawley*?

Even more than that, I've got a problem with the idea of a *City by the Sea*. To citify a seaside town in this country is to totally disregard the special nature of the British coastal resort. From Bournemouth to Blackpool, be they coarse or genteel, they all have a certain something in common; namely, their very outdatedness, their lack of everything – graft, overcrowding, pollution – that makes a city a city. And exactly what is so great about living in a city, when every last survey on the subject tends to show that while around three-quarters of all town and country dwellers express satisfaction with their quality of life, this plummets to around 10 per cent when you ask urbanites? You don't even have to read about it. You can see them promenading along Brighton seafront any weekend from April to August

– thousands of Londoners set free for the day, blinking and smiling with surprise at *all this light and space*! Poor little mole-people above ground at last!

And even when the pier is jammed solid with seething humanity, they're not seething in a *bad* way, as in 'about to lose it'. There's rarely the nastiness you see in similar city situations, even on a Saturday night, simply because the ever-present sea and the incredible horizon reminds us what a big place the world is, and that we are not necessarily condemned to live and die in a rat-run. That's why three out of four properties in B&H is sold to a Londoner; that's why most people who haven't been drained of all hope and high spirits want to live here one day.

And how did we – or rather the council – react to what should have been such a source of civic pride? Why, we flung the bouquets gaily aside and scampered off to spend thousands of pounds of local taxation – which would have been so much appreciated by the old, poor and handicapped, unable to share the seaside dream – on persuading Her Maj to wave her magic wand and turn us into *the very thing that most people want to escape from* – a city. There's logic! Like being Cinderella as the belle of the ball, and volunteering yourself to be turned into a scullery drudge. Frankly, wanting to be a city strikes me as being about as sensible and life-affirming as wanting to be a wart; there could even be a new word for such wanton self-immolation – *citycide*.

So while England's only Grade 1 listed pier continued to crumble slowly into the sea – gone forever, now – while the seagulls grew fierce and fat on all the uncollected rubbish left rotting in the street, and while Brighton schools rose ever higher in the bullying and underachievement leagues, money was thrown ceaselessly at the city bid. And why? Someone I know had the wit to corner Simon Fanshawe, the figurehead of the bid, fresh from his victory breakfast, and ask him – basically – *what had been the point?* Fanshawe glared at the sheer impertinence of the question before blurting, 'Well, the point is that now we can start *talking* about Brighton in a whole new, *different* way!' Well *done*, Simes! I'm sure that's been a real comfort down the years to the old dears in deep Hove who've just had their hip operations cancelled for the nth time; you hero, you!

Indeed, the excitement of certain local politicians over the city bids was a revelation to behold; individuals who had previously been unready, unwilling and/or unable to garner any extra enthusiasm or cash in order to improve mere bagatelles such as health and education were now wetting themselves with righteous fervour at the thought of getting new headed notepaper! And here's where the big picture pans out. The Labour council which took power over this town in the mid-1990s, and still has power today, is a *very* New Labour council, and has been led by thwarted idealists, amongst others, who in the political wilderness of the Thatcher years mutated into strange, free-falling beings to whom power was not a means to an end, but an end in itself.

In short, they became Pod Politicians; like their big brothers in government proper, they still went on about social justice and the brotherhood of man, but inside they'd gone all cold and creepy. Peter Mandelson is, of course, the greatest example, and in his irresistible rise from Lambeth councillor to Chief European Commissioner for Straight Bananas serves as a lesson to all ambitious local bean-counters. They say that politics is show business for ugly people, and in not one word or deed of Randy Mandy's have I ever been able to discern exactly why he chose to be in politics apart from the fact that he isn't personable enough to make it in showbiz, which is obviously his first love; every time I see Dale Winton I want to shout, 'You've got Peter Mandelson's life – *give it back to him*!'

It's common wisdom that though politics may be, like, rotten and corrupt and whatever, it *is* undeniably a profession for grown-ups; moreover, for those who were *born* grown-up, those rare beings amongst us who were quite happy to put fun on the back-burner and go to endless dull meetings when the rest of us were dancing round our handbags in the pleasure dome of youth. But more and more I'm starting to believe that politicians are generally *less* mature than most of us. And that this is because they missed out on the giddiness of youth when they had it, and are seeking instead to have their silly, show-offy salad days *now* – at our expense. Swanking wallflowers, the lot of them – those horrible brats who used to simper, 'Go on, then – muck about! *But I'm going to be rich and powerful one day and then I'll show you all!*' And now, true to their collective word, on quangos and parliamentary committees and local councils up and down the country, they're making us pay – hitting us in the pocket, where it hurts, for their vile vanity projects galore. The Dome, the city bids, the United States of Europe: we held their heads down the toilets a beat too long, and now it's our turn to suffer.

COUNCIL HOUSING, SALE OF

I was eventually rewarded for my council-contrary ways with a headline on the front page of the morning edition of the local paper, in letters as long as a decent-sized line of coke, BURCHILL FIGHTS FOR THE TENANTS. Mind you, I was cut down to size PDQ when I was bumped off the front of the evening edition by Jeffrey Archer getting out of clinker.

The headline came about because I gave a modest cheque to a local tenant-led campaign group affiliated to the national organisation Defend Council Housing. The nationwide attack on social housing stock by central and local government has been particularly virulent in Brighton & Hove, where the council were not above attempting a sort of half-hearted, class-based ethnic-cleansing-without-violence, wherein families who have been in Brighton for generations – who could probably even trace their lineage right back to Brighthelmstone if they could be bovvered, and if they were that sad sort of bourgeois life-lacker – were encouraged to give up their council homes and be 'resettled' in places as far away as Wales, for a few hundred pounds. The excuse which inefficient councils – under the instruction of, surprise surprise! John Prescott – use for privatising council properties is that the housing stock has been so badly neglected over the years. Excuse me – how long have Labour been in power now? And how much longer are they going to keep blaming everything from chlamydia to cannibalism on 'the Thatcher years'?

The work needed to make homes 'fit' for human habitation, continues this crackpot logic, will come at such a staggering price that if they're not sold off to private concerns, the only way to pay for the 'necessary improvements' would be to hike up council rents to an astronomical degree. We can only presume that the types behind such reasoning were a posse of crazed Hyacinth Buckets – or at least Peter Mandelsons – with a hardcore my-home-is-my-showhouse mentality; Defend Council Housing believes that the £650 million 'bill' quoted for Brighton alone is a lie, and that most council tenants are satisfied with their homes and do not necessarily nurse the burning desire for landscape gardening and digital television that this figure presumes. The examples DCH gave me of elderly people in particular, terrified that they will lose the houses they have lived in all their lives, touched even my cold black heart.

They're right to worry, too. Even when council housing stays in the hands of housing 'trusts', evictions of tenants rises by more than a third, rents are more than a quarter higher and management costs around 40 per cent higher. As the chief executive of one such organisation helpfully put it: 'We're a business and our divisions are expected to make a surplus.'

Nothing, it seems, is going to get in the way of the pro-privatisation lobby and their lust for profit. In the spring of 2006, Defend Council Housing Brighton reported that, not content with spending millions of pounds of public money attempting to con council house tenants, some among them were methodically going round tearing down the anti-privatisation posters which tenants put up in their own blocks. Oh, and to sweeten the pill, these charmers were also planning to spend another £25,000 of public money on a video telling the tenants to lie back and enjoy it – just the latest incidence of government, both local and national, robbing Peter the Pauper to pay Paul the PR man.

To sum up, it is very hard to see this apparent loathing of the working class – and the stripping of their assets in favour of the slippery, shape-shifting capitalist, which even the party whose name brags of honest, straightforward toil, Labour, now indulges in as a matter of course – as unconnected to the chav phenomenon of the past few years. The rise of this word mirrors the almost pathological, sexually driven (well, D.H. Lawrence *did* say that only the working class experienced complete orgasms, so maybe the bourgeoisie are right to be jealous) loathing and demonisation of the working class as the only underdogs it's safe to pick on now that race relations and religious hatred laws have made poking fun at any other ethnic group beyond the pale. How ironic, therefore, that in the shameful list of 'chavscum' insults, 'council' is up there with 'pram-face' and 'chip-shop' as a description of working-class people. And ironically, it is such an *appropriate* insult – that is, when not aimed at low-earning, hard-working council tenants, but rather at skiving, money-wasting council members.

In a pleasing postscript to all these trangressions – pleasing for me that is, not for the poor sods who had to suffer – a headline in the Brighton *Argus* of 14 June 2006 blared CULTURE OF 'FEAR AND BULLYING AT COUNCIL'. Turns out that 'institutional racism' within the council was creating 'a culture of fear' which was actually hindering its work in reducing racist incidents. Twenty-one per cent of staff said they had experienced bullying and harassment; said a council worker, 'Members of the public would be shocked to know what's going on at the council. There is a culture of fear that permeates the whole organisation. There is a real fear of coming forward because staff who raise issues become the problem; it doesn't help anyone and inevitably ends up at tribunals.'

Maybe they could give themselves a grant. And in the meantime, stop lecturing the rest of us about how to behave decently. How funny is it to think that the white working class generally reviled by Labour councils as xenophobic and racist probably extend far more tolerance to their colleagues and neighbours of various ethnicity than this holier-than-thou nest of PC vipers!

SILICON IMPLANTS: THE STOPPABLE RISE OF THE NEW MEDIA

(All indented quotes in this chapter are genuine comments posted by members of the Brighton New Media mailing list in 2006.)

> Plumbers, Dentists, now why didn't my careers adviser push me that way . . .'yes, electronics and computers is a growth area right now, all very new and exciting and will be huge in the 1990s, but by the time you're forty, all the action will be in China and the Indian subcontinent – you'd be better off going into dentistry or plumbing . . .'

What is 'New Media'? Computers and that, innit. There was a time when people who did that sort of work would simply say, 'I'm in computers,' but computers have become ubiquitous in so many different kinds of workplaces over the last fifteen years that this no longer sounds remotely impressive to anyone. 'New Media', on the other hand, is an admirably succinct way of saying, 'I created everything you still struggle to understand, and am about to create something so incomprehensibly magnificent it will leave you wailing in the dust like the savage you are.'

It's a phrase that speaks of bleeding-edge Thinkpads and winking plasma touchscreens, blue-sky thinking and stratospheric bonuses, blasting into the office on laser-guided jet boots and joyriding the information superhighway with a bevy of obliging robotic concubines.

Generally speaking, though, that isn't what these people are really doing. Most of them aren't even making games (lots of which are rubbish anyway) or educational programs (lots of which are little more than books with buttons) – they're doing DIY superstore websites, civil servants' training programmes, menus for giveaway DVDs, afternoon TV red button content and Robbie Williams videos. In a market where every product available must either contain a computer, connect to a computer, or have its own website, opportunities to devise this sort of tedium have become as commonplace as grief, yet thanks to the vague cachet granted by that 'new media' tag – hey, you always *said* you wanted to do 'something in the media', right? – the industry is never short of new recruits.

Ah, the joys of that first interview: the office looks clean and classy, the people are young and dress like your friends, perhaps there's even an old Space Invaders machine in the 'rec room', but give it time, give it time ... They'll soon have you weeping with boredom as you amend the same string of code for the eleventh time because they changed their minds about the size of the 'OK' buttons again, or trying not to shriek wildly as they demand, at the end of a twelve-hour day, that you replace every instance of 'Click Next to Continue' in a 200-page program with 'Select Next to Advance'.[1] And if you ever actually get to have a go on that Space Invaders machine – at the Christmas party, say – it will swallow your money and then not work.

But what of the other bold young visionaries who rise to meet these challenges day after interminable day – who are they, and

---

[1] And you can't just do a Find/ Replace All because every page with questions on says, 'Click Next to Continue Your Learning', and they want that left in.

to what end? I do so hate to generalise but never mind about that now: most of them are in their twenties or thirties, have closely cropped hair or heavy metal ponytails, wear Carhartt T-shirts and combat trousers, brandish iPods, go 'travelling' (never on holiday) somewhere in Asia for a couple of months a year, tend to ignore politics, find David Hasselhoff, Mr T and poor little Gary Coleman from *Diff'rent Strokes* endlessly hilarious, cherish 'old skool' trainers and first-generation video games, pay scant regard to spelling or grammar, evangelise about sushi (or manga), go to the Big Chill festival because they couldn't get tickets for Glastonbury, discuss old children's TV programmes and discontinued confectionery products at parties, respect the Rat Pack but wrongly prefer Frank Sinatra to Dean Martin, watch Japanese anime films and freeze-frame all the dirty bits, and enjoy their jobs less than they'd like to admit.

Sorry if any of this sounds a bit harsh: I appreciate that none of the above activities constitutes an actual criminal offence, and several of them are even regularly enjoyed by your correspondent (though I'd sooner die than say which). I should also admit that my own years as a mouse jockey have brought me into contact with some of the nicest, most interesting people you could ever hope to meet. Others, though, are simply tossers.

> I've done shows with Ambulance (planet mu), Decal (rotter's golf club), Rob Rowland (D1), Herv (risc), Numbers (tiger-beat6), New York City Survivors (DUM), Colleen (leaf) & Chris Clark (warp). At the moment I'm trying to build my own website and failing miserably due to distractions from my new copy of Live, a nasty penchant for hazelnut lattes and Edward Harris records.

They just can't help showing off, you see. When it comes to showing off about DJing (as above ... I think), or being arty, or having kids, the explanation seems relatively simple: some people *need* to keep mentioning all the pleasant, worthwhile things in their lives just to block out the hellborn inanity of what they do for a living. Nothing wrong with that! For one thing, it's surprisingly easy to ignore. More annoying are the ones who bother you with group/'team' emails parading the wealth of their knowledge about nanotechnology or the films of Akira Kurosawa for no readily discernible reason – the Wikipedia[2] crowd. Even with these, though, you generally just think, Well, at least you've taken my mind off work for a few seconds, and I honestly didn't know that about sticklebacks.

What seems a great deal more sinister is when they show off *about being new media people*. For those who are 'client-facing' this is practically part of the job description. Whenever they meet representatives of the accountancy firm or crisp manufacturer for whom they are preparing a website – usually from templates they've already used to prepare several other people's websites – it's a safe bet there will be a number of 'unresolved issues' to sidestep: bits that don't work, basically, or changes that have been requested by the client but not made. If they are to avoid the appearance of incompetence it is essential they impress upon their hapless paymasters, who generally have little knowledge of such matters, the sheer molten *modernity* of the whole enterprise. 'Of *course* it doesn't work,' their puzzled frowns seem to say. 'This technology is so red-hot fresh-out-of-the-box even *we* haven't totally worked out how to use it yet. But what's the alternative, Grandad? We *could* do something more basic, but people would only laugh at you.' When they actually open their mouths it will

---

[2] 'Wikipedia' is an online encyclopaedia created entirely by the show-offs who use it. What happens is a show-off in Brighton who's into, say, drum and bass, puts everything he knows about it into the Wikipedia, so that when another show-off halfway around the world who likes showing off about cars but doesn't know much about music hears people talking about drum and bass he can quickly look it up and show off about that too. The chilling possibilities inherent in the notion of a global community of show-offs all working towards a common goal have only failed to become reality this long because most of Wikipedia's contributors are still tied up in bitter disputes about supposed errata with other show-offs who like showing off about the same things they do.

be to unleash a bit-torrent of the insultingly nebulous buzzwords for which their profession is justly derided,[3] offering, perhaps, to 'ramp up the back-end functionality' or 'make the dynamic architectures more intuitive' – anything to draw attention away from the unwelcome subject of the 'core deliverables'.

In a way there's something quite endearing about a lexicon that often appears to owe as much to childhood Saturdays spent watching *Buck Rogers in the 25th Century* as it does to the spirit of cold-blooded Orwellian newspeak. Only in a way, though – in every single other way it's just incredibly irritating. Unlike the jargon connected to most other occupations, which generally acts as shorthand for frequently used terms or identifies concepts unique to a job, new media jargon is often an active barrier to good communication because nobody is ever absolutely sure what any of it means. Designers use it liberally throughout the blueprint documents for their projects because it helps to impress the clients, but their own junior designers invariably have to work from the same documents; the junior designers consequently spend a lot of time doing things wrong or waiting for clarification from people in meetings, the deadline is missed and the client requests an emergency meeting at which the language used will necessarily be three times more obfuscatory than it was in the first instance – because it sounds, you know, more 'efficient'.

This smoke-and-mirrors approach also extends to most other situations where new media companies are exposed to the scrutiny of people who might be able to give them money. The company I work for recently installed a widescreen plasma TV in the reception area: it does nothing at all but show BBC News 24 all day with the volume turned down. Why would they do this, do you think? So that their employees can linger over the headlines first thing on a Monday morning, despite the fact that such an activity is seldom work-related? So that a handful of motorcycle couriers and Parcelforce operatives can leave the

---

[3] See, for instance, http://dack.com/web/bullshit

office just a little better informed about the situation in the Middle East than they were when they walked in? So that I can come down at lunchtime and switch it over to *Neighbours*? Or so that important visitors see it and think 'These guys are so *now*!' or, just possibly, 'They must be so fucking *rich*!'?

There can be little doubt, of course, that this innovation would have to have been approved at the very highest level of the company, and indeed most of the more extreme kinds of foolishness in the industry as a whole tend to emanate from its upper echelons. The new media 'grunts' who do all the actual work often display a healthy, if guarded, contempt for the grandiose folly and twisted syntax of those who rule them, but this is ultimately of no help to anybody. It might well be possible for a worker to distance him/herself emotionally from the stupidity of a job if it's relatively undemanding, but thinking, 'My boss has no idea' when you're still in the office at 10 p.m. and he's on a yacht in the Maldives is more likely to lead to a fit of impotent self-accusation than a surging sense of personal empowerment. Far better to just push all those angry feelings right to the back of your mind and concentrate on something else, like that recurring fantasy about what life will be like when you have your own little startup firm and *you're* the shit calling the shots. One thing you know for sure is that you'd never waste people's time with all that idiotic management-speak; thank God your years of honest slog at the technical coalface of the industry have taught you to appreciate the importance of clear, concise communication!

> OK, enterprise-business level – you know provision of web/email for SME businesses. I wanted to get away from the possible notion that we were talking about 'my little pony' websites. It was just someone was talking about 6 users accounts and stuff . . . it sounded a bit village!

I'm sorry, but it's true: one way or the other, they *will* get you to talk funny. And that's only one of many strange behavioural tics you're liable to pick up. You may find, for instance, that sitting for hours in an open-plan office where every other employee of the company can hear everything you say leads you to regularly communicate via email with people sitting right next to you. This can be fun, at first, because it's almost like being telepathic: a colleague annoys you so you e-denounce them to some nearby friends, who smile their agreement a moment later in full view of the object of your scorn. Honour is satisfied without anyone's feelings getting hurt − it isn't surprising that so many of the telepathic societies that crop up in the realms of science fiction have no concept of This Thing You Humans Call War. There is a downside, though. Damaging conflicts are left unresolved, wanky behaviour is left uncorrected, and gradually, pretty much without your noticing it, you find it less and less easy to actually tell people, in person, what you really think.

This might not be an altogether unsatisfactory development as far as your boss is concerned, but you should keep an eye on it all the same. The more time you spend in the office the harder it becomes to formulate a response to anything outside it; slowly but surely, the world outside your Windows starts looking bigger and scarier than it has any right to be. Perfectly commonplace sights and scenes are transformed into grotesque harbingers of moral apocalypse:

> If you go to Lancing in the evening you'll see there's a number of youngsters cruising around in their converted Novas, while the rest gather outside the mini-market / kebab house / indian ... From what I can see this has actually got worse since I lived in Lancing − much bigger groups of kids than there used to be.

In time, this anxiety can curdle into something quite unpleasant, and quite unexpected when you consider how many of the people involved are, to some degree, middle-class, university-educated oatmeal gobblers. It curdles into hatred − hatred of the poor, the homeless and anyone else whose desperate personal situation threatens to make cross-platform synergy look somehow unimportant. It's no coincidence that the rise of the new snobbery, which brought us epithets like 'chav' and 'pram-face', has been an Internet-driven phenomenon. Supposedly sophisticated people with links to the actual media started it, in a weirdly gratuitous way (popbitch.com was, after all, supposed to be about music industry gossip), but it was the embittered new media pantywaists who picked up the torch and ran with it, in dozens of offensively unfunny websites like chavscum.com (whose shop offers a revealing choice of T-shirt designs: 'Land of ASBO Glory' or 'No, I won't fix your bloody computer'), chavworld.co.uk, chavtowns, chav-dating, chavolympics, etc., etc. What a clever use of all that hard-won expertise, eh? Those kids who keep taking the piss out of you outside the mini-market will think twice next time, now they know what you're *really* made of! Oh, wait – you forgot to put your name on it.

> There is no class snobbery in calling people chavs. Chavs are chavs because they practice [sic] chavvery, they are proud of it, and they are scum. Chavs need to be wiped off this earth, I have had enough of them.

What makes it all even more depressing is that these childish outbursts are actually the nearest many new media types ever get to any kind of social awareness. Even when their own colleagues are the ones in trouble, insular self-absorption remains the keynote. You might think that working in an industry with little in the way of external regulation, governed mainly by the whims of lone egomaniacs who regularly make impossible demands of their employees, would encourage people to look out for each other a bit more than usual, but no. Unionisation is practically unheard of in the new media sector, despite energetic attempts by the GPMU (now, inevitably, part of Amicus) and others to gain a foothold. This could well be just another of the ways in which these thrusting young mavericks express their distaste for the 'rigid frameworks' that made gainful employment such an insufferable drag in their parents' day; it may also represent an unspoken declaration of faith in the future saleability of their own special talents. Even where this is the case, however, it also seems to have rather a lot to do with being scared shitless of upsetting the boss.

In 2001 the CEO of one Brighton new media firm of my acquaintance made nearly two-dozen employees redundant as a result of 'changes in the global economy'. What this essentially meant was that they were still making money – with several million pounds still in the bank – but not quite as quickly as they used to. Fearing the disquiet this might cause the shareholders and anyone who might have been thinking of buying the firm, it was only natural that the CEO (let's call him, oh . . . 'Charlie') should opt to make up the shortfall by setting loose a few of those pesky salary-hogs – or rather, by getting someone else to do it for him. And so, on what had seemed like a perfectly ordinary morning, people started getting unexpected phone calls from the Financial Controller, inviting them to see him in his office. Once there, they were summarily told to clear their desks and leave the building as soon as possible.

If this approach had been calculated to minimise the risk of embarrassing and potentially disruptive public scenes, it failed. Within minutes of the first sacking every single person in the building knew exactly what was going on, but no one had any idea how many more people would be going or who they'd be. Not a phone could ring that morning without draining the colour from someone's face, and no one who picked up and found the F.C. on the other end could be in any doubt as to what would shortly be happening to them. The results were not tidy.

Because it's never easy to concentrate on designing a management training module while a colleague sobs hysterically in your ear, very little work was done that day. In the end, though, this only made those who were spared feel even stupider for not walking out – or at least doing *something* – while it was all still going on. As the full scale of Charlie's actions became steadily more apparent, his remaining employees grew increasingly restless. Many began to whisper the 'U' word.

Someone got in touch with the GPMU, who sent a representative to address the mutineers at a thrillingly secret meeting after work one night. He assured them that what Charlie had done contravened employment law, and that he would never have dared pull such a stunt on a fully unionised workforce. The way forward, it seemed, was simple: they should all join the GPMU and organise a vote over whether to seek full union representation, with shop stewards and all the trimmings. There were a few dissenting voices – mainly people with a reflexive distrust of unions per se – but even most of those seemed to accept that there was no other practical way of keeping Charlie from treating them like cattle again. Desperate times did indeed call for desperate measures; as far as it was possible to tell, they were solid.

Needless to say, news of these intrigues soon reached the ear of the man himself. He took it badly, sulking at home for days on end and using their 'ingratitude' as an excuse to finally accept a large bonus he'd declined for the good of the company the previous year. When he did eventually return to work, those employees he'd identified as the ringleaders of the unionisation bid found themselves getting unexpectedly called into his office at odd hours of the day for intimidatory eyeballings. Charlie made it very clear to anyone who'd listen that he'd resign immediately if the unionisation went through.

In franker moments he'd readily admit that this was mainly because a company with a strong union presence would be harder for him to sell. That didn't prove to be much of a vote-winner, though, so he was forced to fall back on a string of absurd scare stories about unions and the terrible harm they might do to his employees' happy working routines: they won't let you do overtime! They'll create a climate of mutual suspicion between the workers and the management! They'll make you take breaks, even when you don't want to! His employees' telepathic replies were unequivocal: *they won't let us do overtime at the standard rate any more – you'll finally have to start paying us extra for it! We couldn't possibly be more suspicious of you than we are already! A break? Ooo, I'm desperate for one – tell 'em thanks!*

But then he at last did something quite clever. Instead of simply continuing to oppose the unionisation, he began to promote an alternative: the Staff Council. The idea behind this was that each 'team' would elect a representative, and all the representatives would meet at regular intervals to discuss their 'team's' concerns; if unanimity were reached over any particular issue it could be taken straight to Charlie, who would, of course, listen very carefully and take immediate steps to remedy matters – assuming, that is, he felt like it.

A thin veneer of democratic procedure could not disguise the fact that such a body could only be as laughably toothless as a champion gurner, but many of the insurrectionists seemed to find his proposal oddly reassuring. Before, they'd been faced with a difficult choice between doing something quite scary – bringing the union in, and facing Charlie's wrath – or doing nothing, which under the circumstances would have seemed a bit too shameful to be countenanced. Now, though, they could choose between the scary something and a new, improved nothing which somehow *appeared to be something*. It was a masterstroke, really; for all his faults, Charlie certainly had an insight into the thinking processes of the apathetic and dull-witted. (I've heard Tony Blair used a similar trick to wean the Labour Party off socialism, but I dare say it's just an ugly rumour.)

Almost immediately, the tide began to turn. The secret meetings continued to be held but numbers fell, and more and more of those who attended were spouting mimsy tripe like, 'We're not being fair to Charlie – think of everything he's done for the company.' It was obvious that these people were determined to get the kind of representation they deserved – no representation at all – and ultimately they succeeded: the final vote went in the Staff Council's favour and the whole matter was quickly forgotten by everyone bar the luckless few who got elected to it. Four years later, Charlie sold the company for an exorbitant sum and disappeared to enjoy the early retirement his staff had all been dreaming of. It seems unlikely that their new owners would ever attempt anything as self-defeatingly self-serving as those unnecessary redundancies (at the end of the day, Charlie just wasn't a very good manager), but of course if they wanted to, they still could.

Oh, but listen to me going on ... At the end of the day it's no worse than most other jobs, and better than plenty. Maybe Charlie was right, and his minions should just have been grateful; at least when one of them got sacked they had an actual desk to clear. A little way down the road, his deadliest rival had people testing mobile phone interactive content on a row of stools in a small, dark shed at the back of their car park.

One wonders if they presented this to the employees concerned as some form of 'extreme hotdesking', and, if so, how long it took for such an outrageous claim to be swallowed. I'd wager that any new media type worth their salt would swallow it a great deal faster than any normal person, because we're primed to think of our jobs as *special*; no one would stand for such conditions on a production line, but as soon as computers are involved it simply becomes a 'new way of working'. It's this very assumption of uniqueness that lies at the root of *all* our idiocy: the silly language, the snobbery, the political complacency, the endless showing off ... But none of this is unfixable. If we could only calm down about the pixel count for a minute and recognise that we're still basically doing boring office jobs, we might just be able to stop looking down on more traditional professions long enough to claim the sort of rights they've been enjoying for years.

I only mention all this because new media is quite the big noise in Brighton these days. Our first conspicuous success story was Victoria Real, a company which started out selling skiing trips to university chums with souvenir videos as a sideline and ended up designing the *Big Brother* website (which makes an odd kind of sense, when you think about it). To many, VR's growing 'hotness' was inextricably linked to its location; Brighton has long had a reputation for being young, creative, individualistic and – dare I say it – 'funky', and these are exactly the qualities nine out of ten budding new media doyens aspire to project. Add to that the promise of cheaper labour and (from 2000) lower leased line Internet rates than were available in London and the town was soon looking irresistibly attractive to the capital's young computurks, who duly swarmed down to create plucky little startups with meaningless names and achingly quirky mission statements. Someone, and I don't know who although I'd certainly like to, coined the phrase 'Silicon Beach'.

Our local government was, perhaps understandably, delighted by the whole business, and rarely missed an opportunity to associate itself with the new arrivals. It was actually quite surprising how often people from the council found time to add their comments to puff pieces in the *Argus* about this or that new media firm being given some award or winning a big contract (the phrase 'the challenges of the twenty-first century' was never far away). Of course, it was part of their job to safeguard our economy and bring new employment opportunities into the area, but was that really all there was to it? We need only look at Mr Tony Blair's long history of botched IT initiatives for evidence that even our highest-ranking politicians can happily abandon their reason in the name of new technology. I'm sure this has nothing to do with the fact that most of them are middle-aged and look a bit knackered yet are required to convince people that they *understand the future* . . . Perhaps it's a hormonal thing.

In February 2001 a poster bearing the slogan 'Welcome to Silicon Beach: Digital media pier to pier' appeared on a billboard at Brighton Station, funded by two small multimedia companies and one small PR firm which thought small multimedia companies were nice. Speaking at the poster's 'unveiling', Simon Fanshawe said, 'Brighton and Hove are now the birthplace of ambition and success.' Two words in this statement seem especially interesting: the first – 'are' – proves that even Fanshawe, at this late stage, found it hard to think of Brighton and Hove as anything other than two separate places. The second – 'now' – demonstrates his complete disregard, and by extension the disregard of the council for whom he was more or less an unelected representative,[4] for Brighton's whole long history of ingenious adaptability and spontaneous self-improvement, apparently less significant than a single advert that was gone a couple of months later and never seen anywhere again.

Still, his words seemed prophetic – for a while, at least. As Brighton's new media snowball gathered pace, Victoria Real developed into its first poke-your-eye-out unmissable success story, moving into a new office of Death Star proportions on Queen's Road amid rumours of roving on-site masseurs and a subsidised bar. Some of the smaller firms, though, were beginning to struggle. The rise in commercial property prices they them-selves had helped to instigate was putting the squeeze on the startups, many of which were finding their project portfolios not quite comprehensive enough to cover the rent. The cost of living in Brighton was also rising as more and more shops, bars and restaurants mustered the nerve to charge 'London prices'; with wages remaining stubbornly provincial, it wasn't long before many of Brighton's brightest young professionals were looking for somewhere else to live.

if you're trying to get out of brighton to buy or whatever there's hurstpierpoint, it's becoming quite a 'trendy brighton overspill' area. i've had two sets of friends who have recently moved out that way because it's cheaper and they want

---

[4] He it was who'd 'led' Brighton's successful bid for city status; the popular view at the time was that the Labour council was grooming him to be its candidate in a forthcoming London-style mayoral election – until the very idea of such an election was defeated by a city-wide referendum (arf!).

somewhere to have babies etc. they all like it lots. no starbucks either!

In May 2001, just months after the big move, Victoria Real announced a wave of redundancies affecting nearly 20 per cent of its workforce; its head of marketing blamed – you guessed it – the global market economy. It was a minor event, really, in the great scheme of things, but Brighton's new media types had grown so accustomed to thinking of VR as an unassailable flagship that the discovery of this structural weakness seemed disproportion-ately worrying. Even people outside the industry were concerned: there was a palpable air of sullen disillusionment about the *Argus*'s account of the layoffs, and no Fanshawe content at all. In February 2003, VR announced that they were considering a move to London, for the simple reason that that was where most of their clients were. Shortly afterwards they were away – I couldn't say when, exactly, because it seems the *Argus* just couldn't bring itself to report that final betrayal. They've definitely gone, though. I looked in the phone book.

Of course, that isn't to say there aren't still a lot of new media companies operating, and prospering, in Brighton – the 'e-learning' side of things (i.e. civil servants' training programmes) is particularly healthy, with a 15 per cent share of the total UK market. But VR's departure marked the end of the gold rush. The idea, almost plausible in the shadow of their Queen's Road headquarters, that the new media industry might one day be to Brighton what carpet superstores are to Croydon now seems absurd, if not downright unhinged. The practical reality is that Brighton, whether you want to call it a city or not, simply isn't big enough to offer long-term growth prospects to an entirely new economic sector. With the protected land of the Downs all around us and a great big slice of sea in front there's very little room here for many more 'business parks', and the ongoing wholesale conversion of former commercial premises into residential developments only puts office space at even more of a premium. In that sense it was always inevitable that we'd start pricing ourselves out of the market almost as soon as these funky strangers rode into town, and we should not be in the least surprised if tart-with-a-heart Fanshawe's torch songs fail to keep them in the saloon.

Speaking to *New Insight* magazine's Andrew Wasley in August 2000, a young new media 'flexecutive' (your guess is as good as mine) working in Brighton said, 'I think it's nice to be in a location that's fashionable, laid back, and an hour away from London, but this could be easily sacrificed – I'd take a business anywhere there is more scope for making money, that's ultimately what business is about.' Gosh, really? So you mean it doesn't matter how much we flatter or encourage you, you won't ever feel the slightest twinge of loyalty towards us? Jeez – maybe next time we should help out someone with a little more gratitude, like the homeless or the elderly, or any of the hundreds of businesses that would never leave Brighton in a million years because they absolutely *depend* on our unique demographic for their livelihoods.

We probably won't, though. While I was writing this chapter (September 2006), the council announced plans for a 'financial and creative business zone' in the New England Street area (widely considered to be the very last part of central Brighton in which any large-scale development will be possible). The 'zone' was recommended by a panel of experts, who claimed that Brighton needs 'to absorb almost 20,000 new employees over the next 20 years if it is to reach its potential'. Predictably, they forecast that around half of these jobs will be generated by the new media industry.

Anyone who's lived in Brighton longer than five minutes will tell you that what this town really needs is more plumbers. Plumbers work for themselves, require no office space, and perform a valuable public service. I hear the money's good, too.

DETOX, RETOX: THE BRIGHTON PARADOX OF HEALTH AND HEDONISM

When I saw the headline of an editorial in the Brighton *Argus* on 19 October 2006 addressing the fact that for the fourth year in a row B&H was the drugs death capital of Britain – ARE WE VICTIMS OF OUR OWN SUCCESS? – it struck me as being rather cavalier in its attitude. I mean, we all know that Brighton likes to party, and that it's like totally easy to score here, but come on! – respect where it's due and all that.

But, on closer reading, it turned out that the piece wasn't bragging about our ability to have fun big-time, but rather that 'generous help for drug users may attract more addicts'. Sort of a 'keep their needles clean and keep 'em keen' effect, in fact, to the tune of £5.4 million a year. Anyway, when I'd finished sniggering/slapping myself on the wrists, I set to thinking – as you do – about the paradox of health and hedonism in Brighton and beyond; the detox/retox syndrome. And as luck would have it, my hometown appears to be the most extreme personification of this syndrome in the whole of the UK.

In September 2006, free blood tests carried out on more than 70,000 volunteers revealed that inhabitants are expected to live longer than almost anywhere else, amongst other things, as they had the lowest cholesterol scores. Three months earlier it was named healthiest city in the UK by a Sainsbury's poll which questioned 2,800 people from around the nation on smoking, drinking, eating and exercise habits. Each participant was given a health rating of between zero and 20 – and residents of B&H scored 8.76, compared with 7.88 in London and 7.78 nationally. The study also suggested that the average resident drinks alcohol twice a week, eats fast food 'occasionally' and takes exercise twice a week, as well as being the 'healthiest eaters' in the country, buying more fruit and vegetables than anywhere else. It doesn't take into consideration how much of this gets chucked away, however; knowing how keen we are down here on impressing each other, I couldn't help but think of Maggie Smith's line from *A Private Function* as she opens a much-desired tin of ration-book cling peaches and throws them into the communal pig mulch in order to impress her wealthy neighbours – something like, 'I wish we had some glacé cherries to throw away, that would show those stuck-up characters that we regularly have cocktails!' One can equally imagine the healthier-than-thou holistic housewives of Hanover gaily throwing goji, acai and noni – berries, but come to think of it, in Hanover those could easily be offspring – into the communal street compost heap just to prove how up to date they are on the latest superfoods.

So much for the detox, now comes the fun bit: the retox. Not only did the *Argus* claim at the end of 2006 that one in fifty people in our city between the ages of 15 and 64 indulge in crack cocaine and/or heroin, which frankly I just don't believe. (I've been to parties all over this town in the past eleven years and no joker has ever offered me either.

Or maybe, as I've long suspected, all but a precious few of my Brighton friends are tighter than two coats of paint and were keeping their drugs to themselves, the tight bastards!) Not only have we snatched the OD Trophy from the clammy hands of London and Glasgow four times in a row (though the deaths are always around the forty to sixty mark; considering the tens of thousands of people who take drugs here each year, is that really a lot?). Additionally, 2006 research for National Men's Health Week found that 53 per cent of B&H boys suffer 'stress' at least once a week (as opposed to 48 per cent in London!), 'making them feel depressed or anxious'. Almost a quarter of these feebs claimed to suffer stress several times a week or every day! (But, to be fair, it *is* quite a hard decision for a guy to make, whether he should have that first spliff of the morning on Brighton or Hove beach.) Furthermore, in order to deal with the skull-crushing, mind-numbing responsibility, pressure and stress of spending most working days surfing the Internet for 'candid' shots of Jessica Rabbit/Betty Boop sans knickers when they're supposed to be testing Cornish-to-Catalan dictionaries or something equally useful, 31 per cent of Brighton men admit to drinking and smoking, 14 per cent to binge-eating and 4 per cent to taking drugs. The poor diddumses!

Hmm . . . I must admit that I'm always a tad sceptical when I hear some poor soul or bossy-boots trotting out the accepted modern wisdom that drinking/eating/drugging is some sort of escape valve or coping mechanism. Maybe I've been extremely lucky, but when I feel stressed or want to escape I go back to bed with the Fossil sisters (from *Ballet Shoes*, pervert), saving the fun stuff for high days and holidays – which, admittedly, are pretty frequent. The evidence is pretty lame too – when people are *en vacances*, what do they tend to do even more of than usual? Exactly – drinking, eating and/or drugging! Maybe that's just me, but I don't think so.

The simple truth about 'addictions', in my book, is that people do things because they like the way they feel and then are agitated by a pointless and childish Puritanical streak which says that doing something the whole point of which is pleasure is evil, so they then have to pretend that they had no choice in the matter, that they are 'addicted'; that is, they pathologise pleasure. And the argument is as flimsy and inconsistent as it is hysterical; for instance, often newspaper columnists will say that people drink to soothe their frustration because they do mindless jobs with no responsibility or respect. But this is surely contradicted by the fact that doctors and nurses, who have masses of both, have also historically had one of the highest smoking, drinking and drugging scores of any profession.

No, generally people get bent out of shape because they enjoy it, and this is why we find such strong evidence of drug use going way back to a time long before the real or imagined stresses and strains of modern industrial society. Evidence of cocaine use, for example, dates back to 3000 BC in coastal Ecuador, in the shape of figurines of coca-leaf chewers, while in Peru 2,000-year-old mummies were found with bags of coca leaves around their necks. And this is even before the Incas got there!

The British working classes have always been big drinkers – not just the English but the Scots, Welsh and Irish. And all the while, there's been some stuck-up ponce telling us how bad we are. From Hogarth's *Gin Lane* to the *Daily Mail*'s Binge-Drinking Britain, the line is not the hellfire preacher's no-holds-barred, judgemental-with-bells-on *'it's bad!'* but rather the creepy and 'caring' *'it's bad for you!'* And talk about moving the goalposts. During my teenage years, the 1970s, when Britain was allegedly The Sick Man Of Europe – shirking, striking and skiving (those were the days!) more than any other country in Europe according to the *Daily Mail* – we were told that *because* we drank too much, we couldn't/wouldn't work. Now we are The Hard Man Of Europe, working longer hours than our continent-cohabiters, we are told by the same lemon-sucking finger-waggers that we drink like particularly thirsty machines because we work *too* hard, and that we should try to be more like the French – who just happen to be, you guessed it, the current Sick Men Of Europe, economically speaking. And furthermore, we Brits are angry, uneducated apes who, when in liquor, have no interest whatsoever in the civilised Continental model of leisurely sipping a glass of fine wine at a pavement café, while discussing philosophy, planning to bomb unarmed Greenpeace boats and collaborating with the Nazis at the drop of a *chapeau* – gosh, where did *that* come from! – but instead would rather go spoiling for a fight with like-minded zombies. Proles, eh!

And the womenfolk are the worst, of course. From Gin Lane to Alcopops Alley, working-class women – while their more gently raised sisters toy coyly with a Babycham – have shown a disgraceful tendency to enjoy themselves when they're not scrubbing the front step, taking a pasting from him indoors, sacrificing their lives to their thankless off-spring and generally being looked down on by every stuck-up nonce on this sceptred isle. Just look at the shameless hussies – the pop tarts falling out of nightclubs and their dresses in the pages of *Heat* (oh, for the chaste days of Cathy and Claire's sensible advice in *Jackie*, along the lines of 'Generally, it's best to have your clitoris surgically removed when you reach puberty, as retention of it may Get You Into Trouble') and the shop girls doing the same in a high street near you from dusk till dawn any given weekend.

'What do women want?' Freud is meant to have asked. The same as you, Siggy old boy – sex and cocaine, lots of it! Or maybe that's just me. Or how about men making their minds up, for starters – and I'm not just talking about the usual schizoid instructions that a girl should be a janitor in the bathroom, an usherette in the living room and a gardener in the bedroom here. Historically speaking – give or take the odd Sistine Chapel ceiling or two – you could easily be forgiven for believing that the male gender in general consider the only things really worth doing are making money, getting drunk and fighting, in or out of uniform. 'Take an interest in your boyfriend's hobbies!' is the unchanging mantra of agony aunts down the centuries when young women ask for advice on how to keep their dawg on the porch, but when we do, and take up money-making, drinking and fighting with the best of them, do we get any thanks?

No, of course not. We get non-stop grief from them. Before he was exposed as a rutting rotter – not to mention a rotten rutter – the then Home Secretary David Blunkett, fingers no doubt bloodied from a frenzy of Braille *Daily Mail*-devouring, decreed in the summer of 2004 that 'lager loutettes' were shamefully prominent in the anti-social vanguard of vinous vomiters attempting to turn your average British weekend high street into non-stop orgies of sex, sick and fisticuffs. 'They may be the ones to countenance violence rather than calm it,' tut-tutted the Home Sec – you know, that notorious enemy of intoxication and protector of virtue who oversaw a 24-hour licensing law, and under whose aegis a report advocating the legalisation and taxation of prostitution was published; in short, a plan which would make the state the biggest pimp of all, partially living off of the continuing sexual exploitation of thousands of unfortunate working-class indigenous and trafficked foreign women.

Accusing binge drinkers of causing a culture of 'thuggery and intimidation', Lover-Boy Blunkett had a special sharp dig in the ribs for young women: 'It is not chauvinistic to say the presence of women has often been a calming influence in terms of young men starting to lay about each other.' So there you have it, ladies; not only are you expected to slave all working week for approximately a third less money than your male colleagues earn, and do 80 per cent of the housework if you're lucky enough to cohabit with a man, but come Saturday night, rather than letting off steam, you should be prepared to act as his unpaid bodyguard/chaperone/nursemaid too!

Whenever the annual crime figures are published, you can bet that the dear old *Daily Mail* will dust off that old favourite headline of theirs, DEADLIER THAN THE MALE, going on to reveal that women are now responsible for, Ooo, something like 3 per cent of violent crime – up from 2 per cent! While men have seen a massive fall in their proportion of violent crimes, from 98 per cent to 97 per cent. Similarly, there has only ever been the most miniscule rise in violence from drunken women year on year – unless one counts numerous viciously caterwauling assaults on the disco standard 'I Will Survive'.

A drunken woman is more likely to snog you than stab you; though she may well bore you to tears by insisting repeatedly that you are her bestest friend, *ever*! chances are that she won't mistake you for her worst enemy and offer you outside. But a woman's place, it seems, is forever in the wrong. A while ago we were accused of driving men away from the hearth and into the pub with our mindless feminine chatter; now we've done our best to become good drinking buddies for the boys, and we're allegedly ushering in the downfall of civilisation.

Well, forgive me if I don't run for the bunker, but as a member of the gender which has been on the receiving end of violence since time immemorial, I feel beholden to point out that the vile drunks amongst us – the people who use drink as an excuse for everything from beating up their wives to raping their children – are, massively, men. Women may be sloppy drunks, slutty drunks and/or staggering drunks, with a tendency to forever lose one shoe and hold on to their second-best mate like a drowning man running a three-legged race, but they are rarely vile, evil drunks. And I would venture that an ex-Home Sec who came over all holier-than-thou about a bit of ill-advised Saturday night karaoke when two women a week currently die during cosily named 'domestics' is an ex-Home Sec who was no great loss to the nation that surprised him with his trousers down and his guide-dog blindfolded.

Hypocrites and killjoys can try to disguise their envy of young women's newfound freedom as concern all they want, and wring their clammy hands over the damage that binge-drinking can do to their tender young bodies, but one final grotesque fact remains. And that is that a woman is far more likely to be assaulted, raped or murdered in her own home – stone cold sober, an angel of the hearth – by her own husband than she is blind drunk in Babylon by a total stranger. If you're going to put a warning on Bacardi Breezers, logically speaking you should put them on wedding cake too.

This may be why I was slightly bemused when the Council of Her Majesty's Circuit Judges opined that relaxing the licensing laws would lead to a huge increase in domestic violence and rape. Taking into consideration the grotesquely light sentences that the judiciary routinely hand out to rapists and wife-killers, I actually had to stop for a moment on receipt of this information, and work out whether the wiggy one in question considered this a good thing or a bad thing. Not to mention the fact that the more street-fighting between drunken men goes up, as so predicted by our bewigged betters, surely less wife-battering will happen – after all, it's pretty hard to batter and rape when you're sitting in A&E waiting to have your nose sewn back on.

Everybody knows that domestic violence positively flourished in the good old days when pubs were open for exactly half an hour of a Friday night, and many a good honest toiler – not to mention the occasional High Court judge – saw a spot of spouse-smashing as a reasonable way to relax at the end of the working week. And I think judges in particular (and the ruling class in general) might find, if they look into their gnarled black hearts – the gnarled black hearts which habitually seem to believe that it's fine to give a wife-killer a sentence more suited to a litter-bug – the real reason they attempt to give extended licensing a bad rap. Because, basically, you are absolutely horrified that the humble toilers at last – after centuries of slaving away for people like you, sweating blood and tears for every last Saturday and bank holiday we managed to tear from your exploitative clutches – have sufficient time and money with which to enjoy themselves in the way the leisured classes have since the year dot: by getting intoxicated and having sex. And that they're too hungover to tug their forelocks when they see you swishing down the street in your girly gowns the morning after. And that you might put your oh-so-superior toe in some prole-sick, when the revellers might have been much better employed beating up their women behind closed doors, in the privacy of an Englishman's castle, only to get a pat on the back, a chuck under the chin and a suspended sentence from you.

Sometimes you just can't help feeling that almost every English judge is a Frenchman at heart, when they do things like that – as though the *crime passionnel* was alive and well. Though admittedly that's stretching it to describe one of the numerous murder trials one reads about when a man kills his wife for switching television channels when the football's on and gets six months' suspended. English politicians, too, can come over all French when it suits them; whenever some sad, strange little man of Westminster gets caught with his trousers down, and citizens quite rightly start pointing and laughing, there's always some berk who can be relied upon to start banging on about *la France* and how 'civilised' they are over there about old *l'amour*. 'Why, it's practically mandatory for men to have mistresses in France,' they chuckle reassuringly.

Well, someone has obviously failed to inform French women of this, because a few years back France Telecom was forced, at great cost, to discontinue issuing itemised bills after thousands of affairs were revealed to enraged wives who, clearly, weren't privy to the fact that, for a Frenchman, adultery is as natural as, um, collaborating with invaders and blowing up Greenpeace vessels. The fact is that Frenchwomen have always had to put up with a wagonload of crap because, as befits this pathologically prosaic nation, the marriage contract is literally that: no matter how badly a woman is treated, she will find it hard to obtain a divorce unless her husband agrees to it. This supposedly sophisticated agreement actually shrouds a good deal of pain and deceit, and is responsible for a stratospheric rate of illegitimacy in a country that, like Catholic Ireland, nevertheless stigmatises illegitimate children severely.

The 'civilised' nature of the traditional French marriage has always been a by-product not of enlightenment but of repression; France, don't forget, is a country with fewer female members of parliament than most other Western European nations – they didn't even get the vote until 1945 – and also has one of the highest levels of male-on-female violent crimes in the region. The hypocrisy and sham of French marriage, in fact, pretty well sums up France itself: a country where appearance is all, and where the truth is seen as an ill-mannered interloper with no sense whatsoever of *comme il faut*. The French traditionally dismiss us as a nation of shopkeepers, but can anybody think of another country so pathetically bereft of things to boast about that the right to cheat on their wives is their main contemporary claim to fame?

Despite this – or because of it – Frenchwomen are frequently used as a refined, discreet, ultra-skinny bread-stick with which to beat supposedly sloppy, drunken, overweight Englishwomen. But frankly, what's the point in being a perfect, sober size 10 from pubescence to the grave – as in *Frenchwomen Don't Get Fat* – if you end up so boring to be with and so unworthy of respect that your nation's men take an absolute pride in playing away? Similarly, the man *dans la rue* across the Channel is used as a blunt instrument which the finger-wagging lemon-suckers in this country use in an attempt to bludgeon the fun-loving, hard-drinking Britproles down to their own level of repression and boredom, but, just as with their ideal French-women who nevertheless get cheated on left (Mitterand), right (Le Pen) and centre (the rest of 'em), the ragged reality doesn't even begin to stand up to the Francophile fantasy. The stratospheric levels of alcohol-related death, drunken violence and drink-driving in France paint a vastly different picture from the good-humoured, pink-cheeked, always-drinking-never-drunk Eden of popular middle-English imagination, too. Add this to a crap economy and an ever-present tendency to vote fascist when the going gets tough, and a little Saturday night fighting down West Street doesn't seem so bad after all.

Yep, give me the English way of 'avin' it – detox, retox – any day; call it binge-drinking if you like, but at least your liver gets a chance to get back on its feet between bouts, rather than be assaulted on a drip-drip basis day in, day out. It's always been the working-class way, saving your units up for one big gorgeous binge; you can't really have a couple of drinks at dinner-time when you're working with machinery the way you can if you're pen-pushing either side of lunch.

And there's just something so fine about a life lived alternately stone cold sober and blind drunk; it seems so much braver, so much more joyous, somehow, than having a dreary old couple of units a day to take the edge off a life which you obviously find really dull and draggy but don't have the guts to change. Hearing Hard-Fi singing their magnificent anthem 'Living For The Weekend' from the balcony of the Brighton Centre in the summer of 2006, I remember thinking that not for a million euros would I have swopped my brutal, binge-drinking Britain for some mistily sepia, mildly sozzled Provence idyll:

Oh, I've been working a week, I'm tired
Yeah, I've been working a week and I'm
Just living for the weekend

Got some money I just got paid
Got some money and I can't wait
At six o'clock I'm out of here

Working all the time
Work is such a bind
Got some money to spend
Living for the weekend
When it gets too much
I live for the rush
Got some money to spend
Living for the weekend

My people, right or wrong, sicking up all over their shell suits and loving it.

Of course, health and hedonism are not always mutually exclusive. A really good sex sesh can send your immune system shrieking off the scale. A good laugh can lower your blood pressure. And then there is that ideal setting for both sex and laughter, preferably at the same time while stuffing chips into one's gob – the lido.

If there's one thing I love that doesn't make me fat, make my nose bleed or give me cystitis, it's lidos. Lido – even the word is blue-green and shimmering. More than parks, more than pubs, more than Girls Aloud getting out of cabs going commando, lidos seem to me to be the greatest expression of a very public hedonism. And uniquely, they make people healthier, too, without ever once making them boring or self-righteous – as the pursuit of health is so tragically apt to do. As the mayor of Wandsworth said, unveiling London's largest lido and Europe's biggest outdoor pool, Tooting Bec, in 1906, they are 'a means of affording pleasure, stimulating health and warding off disease'.

Lidos are attractive and accessible to all, regardless of age, sex or social status, whereas at every other source of entertainment, from the theatre to football, you can get a better seat by having more money or by knowing the right people. Even though Iris Murdoch dismissed swimming pools as 'machines for swimming in' and said that lidos are 'grander', I see in them the rare sunny side of socialist-democratic culture. Tellingly, most were built in the 1930s when the working class began to enjoy reduced hours and paid holidays at long last.

At a lido, there are no reservations and no complications; wherever you lay your towel, that's your home. Indoor swimming baths make people feel cramped and corralled and sweaty and supervised; swimming takes us back to our soupy, primeval state, and when done inside it merely rubs in just how far we have come from our early grace into an alienated and lumbering maturity – little wonder that pool rage has been reported at some indoor baths in London. But under the sun of an increasingly long hot English summer, the lido makes you feel baptised, blissed out, born again. Will Self once memorably said that orgies are so depressing because there is always a naked fat man eating ham alone on the stairs, but there are no such wallflowers at the lido. There, everyone finds their place in the sun.

This being so, of course, it makes perfect sense that lidos are in the process of being wiped out. With the same local-council logic that sells books out of libraries while subsidising the Internet – what lonely outsider wants to read novels, after all, when he could be learning how to make nail bombs instead? – a shocking number of lidos have been ruined or closed down over the past two decades. In 1990, there were 120 lidos in the UK; today, there are fewer than 50.

Local councils are generally responsible for maintaining the pools when they aren't in use, and problems can arise when those councils lose interest – after all, maintaining a beautiful building which gives pleasure to thousands of council-taxpaying people each year is a bit of a non-starter when you could be spending, oh, £150,000 on a failed European City of Culture bid. Indeed, it has often seemed to me in the past that B&H council has been guilty of 'lidocide' – that is, being quite insanely bent on abolishing any rogue patch of water whatsoever. Even though the council claims that in 2001 it spent £300,000 restoring Saltdean Lido.

Saltdean Lido, ten minutes from central Brighton, used to be in my opinion the most beautiful building in Britain. It became our first public art-deco building to be reconstructed – and it wasn't ruined much, as these things go. The original pool was 140 ft by 66 ft, going from 4 ft deep to 10 ft, and was designed to hold 500 people; they've cut about a third off the length, and turned that part into a paddling pool, even though there was a paddling pool already. With impeccable local council logic, they've filled that one in. In the longest, hottest summer of 2006, when my friend Sara and I spent many an enchanted hangover day there, it was hard to see exactly where that £300,000 had gone – the ruined beauty was a scuffed, mossy shadow of its former shimmering self. Whereas once it had made me think of a cruise liner setting boldly out to conquer new vistas with its bright white beauty, now it resembled a brave, broken battleship limping home – a casualty of the Lidocide Wars.

Having said that, we in B&H are lucky to have Saltdean Lido at all; many seaside towns have a sad, rectangular crater on the seafront, like an open grave where pleasure has been buried. It wasn't Tony Blair who started closing our lidos down, but there does seem to be something about them that is the complete antithesis of bland and priggish Labour Lite. For lidos are both opulent and socialistic, encouraging individuals by the hundred to find true happiness by merging into one big faceless, sun-worshipping mob. Unlike the new regime of 'fun pools', where you have to queue constantly to experience exactly the same thrill as the person in front of you (yet separately, thus seeing them as a rival for your time and space), the classic lido is a blank space on which any fantasy may be projected. Above all, they are an open invitation to do nothing – and with time on their hands, who knows what people might do! Wake up to the fact that they're alive, for a start.

In one way, it's obviously a good job that lidos are closing down all across this green and pleasant land, because otherwise the relatively leisured and affluent contemporary working class might be out there having fun. And thus they might not be able to make themselves available all around the clock for scoldings from the monstrous media legions of finger-wagging sticky-beaks who have come up over the past decade, and for shopping for the worthless, overpriced crap they peddle from up there on Cloud Nine, NW3.

Food bores have been with us forever, but in the past epicureans and gastronomes kept to their own kind, and waxed lyrical about stuffing down larks' tongues in the privacy of their own troughs. They obviously got sufficient kicks from their personal obsession to recognise it for what it was – just another taste thrill, literally – and then, appetites satisfied, went off to worship their chosen gods, albeit false ones. Today's food bores, however, in the absence of having any life of the mind or of the spirit, have made what should be a private pursuit into a public crusade: the cult of 'Foodoo'. Foodoo cult leaders – Jamie Oliver and Gillian McKeith come immediately to mind, hectoring horribly – are so narrow-minded and unimaginative (Oliver claims never to have read a book, while McKeith can poke around the excrement of strangers for money and still not see herself as an object of pity) that they have focused on grub as an explanation for all that ails the world. Working-class kids doing lousy at school and the gap between rich and poor in this country growing ever greater? It's not our foul class system and the continuing stranglehold of the old school tie, bolstering up dumb rich kids and keeping down smart poor kids; no, it's *turkey twizzlers*! Put that right and, hey presto, everything's beautiful and everyone's equal!

It's a lie, of course. The nutritional input of growing youngsters is neither here nor there; the Eton mess served up at lunchtimes would cause a riot at Wormwood Scrubs, yet the boys who eat it go on to run the country, as they always have. And when we look at our greatest sportsmen, particularly footballers, they are to a man working-class lads who have grown up tucking into the same trans-fats as everyone else on their estate.

'A healthy mind in a healthy body' goes the old saying. All well and good. But as Peggy Lee – a dedicated drinker who was also a great performing artist – once asked, 'Is that *all* there is?' Look at the great wits and writers since time immemorial – what an all-round smoking, drinking, drugging, troughing tribe they were! Thank goodness that Oscar

Wilde and Dorothy Parker, two great examples of brilliant minds in dodgy bodies, aren't still around to be subjected to the imbecility of the Foodoo Nation: she'd be forced into apologising for her droppings on prime time TV, while poor Oscar would be yelled at by Harvey The Mean Marine as he dragged himself around an obstacle course, one-liners silenced for once. My dear, the indignity!

What exactly is missing in the lives of the followers of Foodoo that they take it upon themselves to worry so obsessively about what other people eat? I don't know if it's cause or effect, or what came first – the corn-fed chicken or the free-range egg – but it is a fact that people who are obsessed with healthy eating are quite mind-blowingly boring to talk to. I for one would rather be stuck in a lift with Oscar and Dottie than Gillian and Jamie.

WINNING OLYMPICS CAN STOP BRITAIN BECOMING A NATION OF VICKY POLLARDS! screamed a *Mail* headline. But my fear would be that a nation of health-bores, obsessively cautious about and fearful of mere food, could never have produced the sick, brilliant minds that produced Vicky, Daffyd, et al. in the first place. And frankly, I'd rather be 'big-boned' than dull-minded – I'd rather put 'junk-food' in my mouth than have boring garbage come out of it. I'd rather sit on my fat ass reading books and eating chocs all day than be as self-righteous and small-minded as people like Oliver and McKeith, who really seem to believe that if the poorly educated and badly paid ate ten portions of fruit and veg a day, society would then play fair with them and their problems would be solved. The simple fact is that you are not what you eat; you are where you're born, you are how rich your parents are, you are where you went to school, and what you are lucky enough to be handed on a plate. Even Ruth Kelly has admitted that the gap of achievement between the richest and poorest children is now bigger than when Labour came to power! The idea that all that is stopping working-class children from achieving is that their dumb working-class parents are stuffing them with turkey twizzlers – rather than the whole rotten system of class, privilege and nepotism – is a sickening and dangerous lie.

And a chub, after all, can lose weight, as I well know. But a life-sucking, fun-crushing bore, alas, is one forever.

As the century progressed, Foodoo Followers became emboldened by the acceptance of their crazed leaders Oliver and McKeith, and their raids on both common sense and a sense of perspective became ever more daring. In a world still plagued by starvation in parts, FFs openly fussed and huffed over the exact source of their food, often demanding that it came from the same county, postcode and, in some extreme cases, from the very same street! Amusingly, these were the exact sort of snobs who ten years ago would have been mocking the English prole abroad for not having any truck with 'foreign muck'; now it's the working class who happily dig into outlandish cuisine while the Foodoo bourgeoisie can't bring themselves to wrap their precious lips around anything which didn't live near enough to the restaurant when it was alive to walk there, before dying a peaceful and natural death in the kitchen, no doubt.

It isn't even just restaurants who go in for this sort of eat-your-nearest-and-dearest fetish these days either. In November 2006 the Brighton *Argus* ran an item, to my mind verging on the grotesque, about how 'A museum is stepping back in time to serve food made from its own pigs. The Weald and Downland Museum is hosting a Pig To Pork event this weekend. Its Tudor kitchen will serve food made from traditional recipes made from pigs bred at the museum, rare breeds including the ginger-coloured Tamworth pigs.' Eww – even the hair colour of the poor porcine being gets a look-in! Am I being over-sensitive here –

there's always a first time! – or is there not something rather repellent about the idea of eating one's own friends/pets/dumb charges?

This is the exactly the kind of don't-do-as-I-do-do-as-I-say snobbish hypocrisy which sees Green Eeyores flying all over the world to climate change conferences which decree that people shouldn't be allowed to take cheap flights as they warm the climate – in short, that only rich people can fly, as was the case fifty years ago. It also leads to rich white people in Western Europe telling poor non-white people in China and India that they shouldn't build dams, drive cars or, in fact, aspire to any of things that make life in the First World so damn enjoyable that every poor sod from the other two worlds is trying to get here.

Of course, when the working class couldn't afford to go abroad, Habitat whores and Elizabeth David disciples found all things Continental desirable and took great delight in mocking the stereotypical Brit family shivering behind their Blackpool windbreaker as a Force 9 gale blew away their 'Kiss Me Quick' hats. Then, when cheap flights made France and Spain accessible to the lower orders, the Hyacinth Bucket Tendency packed up their spades in a huff and ventured further afield, to Turkey, Greece and anywhere else where a torturing fascist junta in power kept prices low and the population docile. In recent years, a combination of distaste for tourists (they themselves, of course, are 'travellers' – that is, tourists who don't tip, the tight bastards) and a desire to be seen not leaving a dirty great carbon footprint in the sky have seen vacationing snootbags come full circle, and now cafés all across the Isle of Wight, Devon and Cornwall, as well as Brighton, have replaced baked beans with bruschetta and shown builder's tea the door in favour of Fairtrade coffee.

But fair to whom? Certainly not to those of us fortunate to be middle-aged and of working-class origin, who always spent our childhood holidays in Devon, Cornwall and the Isle of Wight when no one with money wanted to go there, yet must now get used to sharing these unassuming beauty spots with the braying upper-middles and their vile dyslexic, anorexic brats. When the Foodoo cult leader Jamie Oliver deigned to grace Cornwall's Watergate Bay – a place where I have idled away many a happy afternoon at the burger bar above the surf shop – with the latest branch of his over-priced scram-shop 15, you could hear snobs all across *Independent*-reading England breathe a sigh a relief that Cornwall – that most wild and majestic of English counties – was now 'do-able'. My dear, the restaurants used to actually serve *white. sliced. bread*! – do they want us to get cancer or something?! No longer. As the insufferably-smug-yet-terminally-socially-insecure '*Indy*' brayed in 2006, 'A Jamie Oliver restaurant, an academy for extreme sports' (which has been there for like ten years, incidentally) '. . . Alex Wade visits Watergate Bay, where family holidays are moving upmarket.' In other words, *no fucking proles*! And no blacks, either, I'll bet, at those prices, which is something of a side-benefit, albeit one they'd never dare ask for, for your average somewhat ethnically nervous *Indy*-reader.

Brighton, it must be said – for all its boastful Bohemian-ism – is the worst offender when it comes to Bucket-like behaviour about the sort of tourists it is willing to accept. As far back as 1999, Brighton's then head of tourism, Amanda Shepherd, was looking down her aquiline nose at the idea of anything so coarse as a 'resort': 'There is still a perception that we are part of this traditional seaside resort. I am not in any way being negative about them, what I am saying is that we target different people.' People with fat wallets and no kids, ideally – no dirty day-tripping proles, in other words. Ms Shepherd went on to say: 'Because Brighton is a very tolerant place and a comfortable place for gay couples to come for holidays, the British Tourist

Authority is working with London, Brighton and Manchester specifically on that.' What a strange kind of tolerance! 'We're going to be *tolerant*, particularly of you *rich people with loads of disposable*!'

Hyper-loyal adopted Brightonian that I am, I couldn't help cheering when in 1988 plucky little Bournemouth ran adverts – along the sides of Brighton buses, no less! – winking BOURNEMOUTH: THE RESORT WITH MORE STYLE. In a cheeky and clever retort to Brighton's 'Don't-mention-the-R-word' snootiness, it also went on to win prizes for Best Resort of 2004, for the cleanest beach in the UK in 2005 – scoring 99 out of a possible 100 – and four Blue Flags in 2006 – proving that it is far wiser, not to mention nicer, to welcome all colours of money and not just the pink pound, which, quite understandably, can be as fickle as any other with the cut-price fleshpots of Europe just a hop, skip and a sashay away. After all, tourism here supports 13,000 jobs and injects £380 million into the local economy each year. This being the case, isn't 'Come one, come all!' a rather more appropriate attitude to take than 'Come ABC1s – and the rest of you go to Blackpool.' It ill behoves Brighton, after all, with its singularly blowsy rep, to come over all Bucket and NQOT on this issue; everybody's somebody's chav, after all.

Sometimes it seems that Brighton, in common with every other aspirational brand name in the country, is chasing every sort of money except for the kind earned by hard, thankless labour and then spent modestly on pursuits that don't make a vile mess for some other poor bugger to clean up the next day. The tourism bigwigs of Brighton have spent the past ten years attempting to keep away low-earning, low-spending families in favour of attracting the pink pound and the stag shilling. In an unintentionally hilarious statement combining extreme Bucketism with an admirable lack of concern for the predicted future perils brought about by global warming, the president of the Brighton and Hove Hotels Association, Roger Marlowe, wrote in the *Argus* in November 2006 that hotter summers would see the Sussex coast becoming more like 'Nice or Cannes – the traditional seaside town will become more sophisticated and the day of the kiss-me-quick hats will be finished.'

One can almost hear the sound of two plump white manicured hands being rubbed together in anticipatory relish of snobberies yet to be enjoyed at the expense of the reviled day-trippers. And let's see off the oh-so-chavvy stags and hens too, while we're at it, whose business we trawled for quite shamelessly just a while back. Now it's the older, richer, 'creative' coin our all-fur-coat-and-no-knickers city-by-the-sea seeks – the Menopausal Media Moolah? Got to be me! – and I'm sure they'll get it too.

But – and it's two big buts – be careful what you wish for. And you can't fight Chaos Theory – life will find a way, and so will human beings in pursuit of fun. Brighton started out as a detox town, in 1750, when Dr Richard Russell published his *Glandular Diseases, or a Dissertation on the Use of Sea Water in Affections of the Glands*, prescribing sea water in every form, from swimming in to drinking, mixed with milk – the Olde Worlde equiv of a wheatgrass smoothie, and just as appetising I bet – as a cure for a wide range of ailments. He died in 1759; the plaque on the wall of the Royal Albion Hotel says simply, 'If you seek his monument, look around.'

But if you look around Brighton now – from East Street to West Street and all the way to once-genteel Hove – you see not a detox town, but the most dedicated retox city in the British Isles. We have come full circle, gone the whole hog and are currently living high off it; if global warming continues and the summers to come are anything like the astonishing summer of 2006, there's every chance that given the existing youth-appeal of Brighton we will become more like Ibiza and Ayia Napa than Nice and Cannes – and a good thing too, because who in their right mind wouldn't rather look at gorgeous girls doing it with gorgeous boys for drugs rather than gorgeous girls doing it with dirty old men for money?

' "Take what you want and pay for it," says God', shrugs the elegant old Spanish saying, and Brighton, going on past experience, will surely do that when it comes to retox and detox, pleasure and profit. 'Inter Undas Et Colles Floremus' ('Between Downs And Sea We Flourish') goes our city motto, over two ambisexual dolphins having a right old roll-around – though David Gray, who took most of the photographs for this book, says: 'It should be whatever the Latin is for "We Have It Away By The Sea", and the crest would show two burglars loading an old table into a van, the interior of which already includes a mixed group enjoying multiple acts of love.' Or the Latin for 'It's Too Late To Stop Now', perhaps. Or even, if you halved the dolphins, 'We're Not Here For A Long Time – We're Here For A Good Time'.

And that good time belongs to all, equally – the young and the old, the gay and the straight, the chav and the snob. All of us united in the simple truth that no one with half a heart and a sliver of brain is immune to the call of the wild once in a while, no matter how good a job they think they've done castrating themselves. (In the USA right now, even the singularly sacred cow of American Motherhood is having a right old taking-back-the-tits rebel moment with the wild success of *Mommies Who Drink*, a book which celebrates 'the three-martini playdate'.)

And to all and any of those spiritual eunuchs who would seek to spoil people's fun, whether for reasons of envy, snobbery and/or fear, all masquerading as morality, I will leave you with the following thought on the process of intoxication – the paradox of health and hedonism, if you will – from Stuart Walton's *Out Of It*, the best book ever written on the simple human desire to retox, against all the advice to the contrary that increasingly assails us:

> There is an unquenchable ambition in most of us to have more of whatever it is about life that makes it feel dynamic ... The pursuit of intoxication is no more abnormal than the pursuit of love. The concept of pursuit is the key. It is what ties the acquired drive for intoxication within us to the innate drives for food and water ... As an acquired drive, it is unique. We may lust after glamorous social attachments, the thrills of dangerous sports, the sensuality of power and authority, but only intoxication is pursued with the same sense of imperative as we feel the need to feed ourselves ... If we are biologically predisposed to intoxication, how can we ever be talked out of it?

Stick that in your wheatgrass smoothie and shove it.

OH I DO LIKE TO GUEST ON MY MATES' B-SIDES: OUR GLORIOUS MUSIC AND YOUTH CULTURE HISTORY

As far as most Brightonians would be concerned, it started at the Hippodrome – an eye-wateringly elegant art deco pleasure palace which even today looks as incongruous in narrow, workaday Middle Street as a showgirl at a funeral – but in fact it started at the Essoldo, an eye-wateringly elegant art deco picture palace on North Street which would end up being demolished in 2001 to make way for some sporting goods shops. Outside, where they'd been queuing all afternoon, the frigid air was only tolerable if you stamped up and down, hugged yourself and covered your face with mittened hands. But all this was forgotten in the warmth of the auditorium as it slowly filled with bodies and noise; duffle coats were shrugged off and cheeks took on a rosy glow, as if anticipating the exertions to come.

Those sitting nearest the front found it hardest to sit still. They were forever turning in their seats and craning their necks to see up to the balcony, impatient for it to be full of people because only then could the thing finally begin. But then it *was* full, and *still* it didn't start; the doors were closed and the impatience spread from the front rows to the rest of the crowd, raising the room temperature in time with the pitch of their restless chatter until slow hand-clapping seemed not just appropriate but physically necessary.

The lights went out: every single person in the room leapt out of their seat and screamed the loudest scream of their lives. The stage lit up and there they were, just as they'd been on telly but brighter, sharper and in full colour. Standing in front of the others, *he* shone brightest of all – but then he was the only one anyone really wanted to see. When he opened his mouth to sing, the crowd screamed louder still to drown him out, as if to experience his presence with more than one sense at a time would be to risk some form of permanent damage. It was a sensible precaution: just *looking* at him was making a good many of them sweat and drool and weep and seep in such uncontrollable floods that death by dehydration already seemed a very real possibility. None of them was surprised to find themselves like this – it was expected. Everyone knew that the nerve-shredding joy of coming face-to-face with the star of your dreams could only be tolerable if you stamped up and down, hugged yourself, covered your weeping, snot-streaked face with your hands . . . But this was the first time most of those who were there that night had ever actually done it. It was also the first time anyone had done anything even *vaguely* like that at the Essoldo.

The date was 6 February 1962. The man was Cliff Richard.

Ha! Well, I know – shame it couldn't have been Elvis, eh? But of course he never even played in Britain, let alone Brighton, and however much of a hit he was with British teenagers he was rather too remote a figure to be any real cop as a romantic fantasy or role model. If you lived in Brighton you would not know any Miss Clawdy, nor would you ever have seen a train arrive sixteen coaches long; trying to picture yourself hanging with Elvis would therefore have involved a fair amount of risky guesswork, and this is never an appealing prospect to a jittery youngster in search of a concrete identity. Doing up an old London bus and driving it to France to have a bunch of crazy adventures, on the other hand, was something even the most provincial of minds could readily grasp, and yearn for (I mean, wouldn't it be *brilliant*?). Cliff may have sung with an American accent but he was still unquestionably one of us, and although his reception at the Essoldo was to be topped a couple of years later when a pack of Scousers called the Beatles (sic) played the Hippodrome, he was the first to demonstrate that being a British teenager could, in a naff sort of way, be cool.

For a start it meant you could form your own band – merely a question of picking up the first bulkily bespectacled Shadow with a frozen, sinister grin you found hitch-hiking on the road to Paris – and knock out some tunes yourself. I'm sure there must have been plenty of teenagers doing this in Brighton throughout the late 50s and early 60s, but who they actually were remains a bit of a mystery. And the same is sadly true of most other people who have *ever* started a band in Brighton; at any one time there's always one or two getting signed to major labels and/or sucked up to by the *NME*, but somehow none of them ever quite makes it to the upper mezzanine of stardom. This seems peculiar, given that we have one of the highest student populations in the country, dozens of live music venues and a reputation for being all 'creative' and stuff. When, in 1999, the Brighton and Hove Bus Company hit upon the wheeze of putting a different famous name associated with Brighton on each of its buses, I for one expected to be stunned on a daily basis by hitherto unimagined rock 'n' roll connections – 'What? You mean to tell me *Throbbing Gristle* came from *Peacehaven?*' – but of all the buses in B&H's fleet, just five were named after pop stars.[1] Of these, four were solo artists: Dusty Springfield, Norman Cook (fair enough – they both lived in

---

[1] Great missed bus-naming opportunities: Orbital, Nick Cave (weirdly, lives in Hove), Genesis P. Orridge, Captain Sensible, Wendy James (her out of Transvision Vamp), Gary Clail, Phats, Small.

Brighton/Hove), Leo Sayer (actually a Shoreham boy) and Adam Faith (for no better reason than that he 'often paid visits'). The only actual *band* to be honoured was The Who.

The Who were from London, but for much of the early 1960s they spent their Wednesday nights performing at the Florida Rooms, a 1,500-capacity club connected to the Aquarium buildings on Brighton seafront. They were still calling themselves the High Numbers at the time – they only became The Who in 1964, after which we didn't see quite so much of them round these parts. Their time in Brighton happily coincided, however, with the rise of a new youth cult: the 'modernists', or mods. These were mainly young working-class men who liked expensive suits, Italian scooters, Tamla Motown records, amphetamines and shouting, 'We are the mods, we are the mods, we are we are we are the mods.' Their mortal enemies were, of course, the rockers – mainly young working-class men who liked black leather, motorbikes, trad rock 'n' roll, amphetamines and throwing deckchairs at mods. The Brighton mods generally congregated in up-market coffee bars[2] like the Automat at the Clock Tower, the Scandinavia Bar and the Zodiac; this last just happened to be a short distance down the road from the Florida Rooms.

Inevitably, *some* mods went to see The Who play. That's a given – no one's denying it! But the question of exactly how much any of them actually enjoyed it is still being bitterly contested today. The 'Witness' section of the BBC News website contains dozens of personal accounts of the 60s' mod era, and their only major point of difference concerns whether or not The Who were a 'proper' mod band. 'Colin, UK' claims, 'the Who were the mods' favourite group' and 'Adam, England' appears to concur, but 'Vincent, USA' insists, 'No self respecting mod would have given them the time of day; they were phoneys.' Paul Smith of Hong Kong (quite the globetrotters, these ageing mods) hammers

---

[2] Which seems a bit foolhardy, considering they were already ripped off their tits on speed half the time. When did they ever put their feet up?

the point home with, 'True mods wouldn't have been caught dead listening to The Who', while 'Jerry, UK' somewhat bewilderingly asserts, 'The Who were dressed up by their manager'(?).

Needless to say, references to this controversy are entirely absent from *Quadrophenia* (1979), The Who's rock opera about the infamous bank holiday weekend in 1964 when Brighton beach was overrun with thousands of scuffling mods and rockers (see Timeline). In that film, although the mods are seen to listen to a lot of Tamla Motown, Detroit soul, etc., The Who are unquestionably their favourite band and 'My Generation' is unquestionably their anthem. The party scene, in which the assembled cast pogoes wildly around a suburban living room while shouting along to this admittedly classic song, is as much an elaborate product placement exercise as it is a part of the reconstruction, and the little flickers of authentic embarrassment which punctuate the revellers' fraudulent frenzy suggest that some of them may well be aware of this. Toyah Wilcox brazens it out, of course, but then who's to say, looking back on the complete body of her 1980s work with the enhanced perspective of hindsight, that she ever even knew what embarrassment was?

To be fair, most primary sources seem to agree that, in every other significant respect, *Quadrophenia* is a reasonably accurate portrait of those times. As such, it was always inevitable that the main characters would be Londoners: not only was mod never a Brighton-specific phenomenon, its fixation with slickness and novelty meant it could only really make sense with big-city backdrops. The one Brighton mod in the film, played by *Sting* of all people, is at first worshipped by the others as 'the Ace Face' but ultimately considered a fraud on the basis that he has a (supposedly) demeaning job as a porter in a seafront hotel. Although this is used as a device to make central character Jimmy question his own values, what it means to be a mod, etc., it also reflects what, in terms of the mod ethic, would have been a thoroughly reasonable prejudice – for how can anyone legitimately claim to represent all that is new and exciting from the safety of a traditional family seaside resort? Perhaps 'Colin, UK' puts it best: 'Often Brighton Mods would have punch-ups with London Mods . . . they would come here and pinch our birds because their clothes were always ahead of ours.'

Mods against mods, you say? But I thought – oh, never mind. It's probably inevitable that teenagers/ 'young adults' will always end up fighting more often, and more bitterly, with other members of their own gang than they ever will with outsiders. Mind you, it would've been fun to be a fly on the wall in the Starlight Rooms after 'Itchycoo Park' sent the first turncoat mods peeling away to join the hippies: 'Oi, Jimmy! Did someone throw up on your Fred Perry?' 'No way, man, I tie-dyed it.' 'But it's fucking ruined!' 'Hey, no, it's beautiful – just like you.' (BOP!)

Those few mods who stayed loyal to the cause hung on, getting slowly scruffier and angrier, until the early 70s, by which time they were wearing their hair so closely cropped they became virtually indistinguishable from skinheads. The hippies, of course, hung on and *on* – Brighton is *still* awash with them – but, to be honest, I've no real interest in saying much about them here. Not that I've got anything against them, you understand (in fact, *big* thumbs-up to both the music and the drugs), just that it seems absurd to talk about them as a 'youth cult' when they were clearly nothing of the kind. Youth cults have many defining characteristics, but jumping up and down to loud music and getting into fights with ignorant rivals are, for my money, two of the most important. The hippies liked loud music but it only ever seemed to make them do that eyes-closed, head-wavey thing, *and they specifically said they didn't want a fight.* For about ten years they got their wish; then something unbelievably heavy happened.

When the Sex Pistols hit the charts in 1977, teenagers all over the country were inspired to tear up their clothes, put glue in their hair, start rubbish bands and – crucially – jeer at hippies. In Brighton, early punk activity was largely centred around the Attrix Records shop in Sydney Street (now David's Book Exchange), the Richmond pub (now the Pressure Point) and a poorly converted nineteenth-century burial vault that ran under both the Brighton Resource Centre in North Road and the Presbyterian Church in Church Road. Christened, simply, 'the Vault', this became a combined live music venue and rehearsal space for first-generation Brighton punk bands with burgher-frightening names like Brighton Riot Squad, the Lillettes, the Molesters, Devil's Dykes[3] and Smeggy 'n' the Cheesy Bits. Brighton's run of bad luck in terms of chartbound sounds looked set to continue, but it would be fair to assume that all of these bands had at least a passing interest in making people jump up and down.

There were fights, too: fights with teddy boys (dispiritingly reinstated following the mid-70s' rock 'n' roll craze), fights with skinheads, fights with lying hippies who evidently *had* wanted a fight after all … Almost anyone under thirty who wasn't also a punk, in fact. Even the thickest of the punks were acutely aware of their position as universal scapegoats, and made a show of taking umbrage while secretly revelling in it, but they always set a little time aside to fight amongst themselves. Ex-Brighton Riot Squad member Atilla the Stockbroker, in a piece for the estimable *punkbrighton.co.uk*, recalls how the punk – ahem – community closed ranks over his short-lived ensemble as soon it became clear that their drummer was a teddy boy:

> One of (our) rehearsals in the Vault was noisily invaded by another punk band, the very young, very drunk, more or less all-girl Molesters, plus their hangers-on. 'See – I told you! Brighton Riot Squad have a TED DRUMMER! You WANKERS! You should be BEATING HIM UP, not letting him play in your BAND! And where are your BONDAGE TROUSERS? You're wearing FLARES!!! You're HIPPIES!'

With chutzpah like that on display, it was only ever going to be a matter of time before 'the Man' came a-calling. Word of the new

---

[3] Sounds rude, but actually named after a local beauty spot. You kids!

Brighton bands soon reached the ears of the record company bigwigs, who were at that time in the process of snapping up anything with a spiked wristband following a damaging period of early indecision about whether or not any of this 'punk' nonsense was going to be worth the effort. They held a showcase audition at the Top Rank Suite in West Street, attended by the Piranhas, Nicky and the Dots and – oh yes – 'Wrist Action', amongst others. Anxious to avoid being jostled by rowdies (and in this way entirely missing the point), they insisted that the audition be in private; unfortunately, most of the bands were so unnerved to find themselves performing in the middle of the day to a small group of hippies in suits who had no interest in spitting at them that they played even worse than usual. The only ones who did all right out of it were an obscure combo called Joe Cool and the Killers – who were signed up on the spot and, of course, never seen or heard of again.

The Piranhas did eventually get a contract, and went on to score Brighton punk's only significant chart hit with 'Tom Hark', thanks to the faintly embarrassing attentions of a young Pete Waterman (you know – him off of Stock, Aitken and Waterman). Their sound was lighter and more ska-inflected than was usual at the time, and characterised by a brand of sly humour which still resonates with many Brighton bands today (viz La Frange and the mighty Wonky Beak). They hadn't had an easy time of it on their way to the top: an organised hecklers' union known as the Anti-Piranha League would regularly – often violently – disrupt their shows for reasons that remain unclear (but were probably connected to their appearances at Anti-Nazi League benefits), and they'd recently been involved in a car accident which killed their road manager and hospitalised most of the band. For a while it seemed like nothing could put them down, but, in true Brighton style, getting into the charts caused them to split up almost immediately.

Less successful but generally a bit funnier were Peter and the Test Tube Babies, who can be seen ruining Kemp Town beach for everyone else on the cover of their debut album *Pissed and Proud*. When Elvis Presley died in August 1977, a shocked world turned where it has always turned for solace – to its minstrels – and the Test Tubes rose to the challenge, putting into words what the rest of us were still just barely allowing ourselves to feel on their powerful eulogy 'Elvis Is Dead' (*Elvis had a heart attack/ 'Cos he got too bleeding fat/ He weighed nearly half a ton/ Looked more like a pregnant mum*). Sustained public indifference ensured their longevity; as of this writing they *still* haven't split up, and are almost certainly playing in a dingy pub somewhere near you *right now*.

By the time the 1970s drew to a close, the Vault was beginning to crumble. Its ancient walls had never been intended to withstand the Sound of Young Brighton and were cracking open to disgorge something even more shocking than the 'c' word that had no doubt helped cause the damage in the first place. To begin with it was just the odd femur or tibia every now and then, but as the situation worsened whole coffins, with inscriptions dating back to the 1800s, started sliding through the walls. It's a tribute to the old-fashioned decency underlying the studiedly tasteless poses of the early punks that very few of them relished the idea of sharing rehearsal space with bits of dead people. As Atilla the Stockbroker puts it, 'If all this had happened ten years later I guess the Vault would have become the most popular goth or death metal venue in the world – surely this was the very definition of death metal, or at the very least death punk – but there weren't any goths or death metallers then, and many of us were actually rather uneasy about the whole thing.'

Inevitably, the Man – this time in the form of Brighton Council – stepped in, and the Vault was closed for good.[4] Bands continued to rehearse in the Resource Centre upstairs but in October 1980 this was burned down in suspicious circumstances. To many it felt like the end of an era; punk itself was far from dead, but even its sternest proponents were beginning to doubt its power to effect

---

[4] Just this once, I think the Man may have had a point.

any degree of long-term cultural change. The place it fleetingly occupied in the music charts had already been usurped by the more radio-friendly strains of 'new wave' (to all intents and purposes, punk you could introduce your grandmother to), and it had been comprehensively mocked across the whole spectrum of TV comedy, from the *Two Ronnies* to *Not the Nine O'Clock News.* The time seemed right to move on – but where?

Unfortunately, you couldn't just go around calling yourself a 'new waver' because there was no such thing and you would only have been laughed at. The 'new romantic' trend spawned by groups like Spandau Ballet and Duran Duran in 1981/82 saw many thousands of young men swiping their mums' makeup and worrying about whether they'd pierced 'the gay ear' by mistake, but such behaviour seemed dangerously effeminate to most of the punks (even some of the girls). For them, 'goth' was the only way to go: it was, after all, very much like being a punk, except there was more of an emphasis on moping and you had to do that eyes-closed, head-wavey thing instead of jumping up and down (for *shame!*). It was *huge* in Brighton, with clubs like the Basement and Sister Ray's drawing great legions of chalk-faced miserygutses from the furthest-flung corners of Crawley every Saturday night, but it never seemed altogether . . . seemly here. In a town so overtly geared towards generating fun and diversion, anyone striving to look like a consumptive undertaker whose cat's just died runs the risk of looking like they've missed the point. Even Nick Cave, legendary founder of Australian goth favourites the Bad Seeds, seems to have recognised this, as anyone fortunate enough to have seen him sallying forth down New Church Road in his dayglo-orange romper suit will gladly attest.

The only other cult to mop up significant numbers of defecting ex-punks was mod. That's right, you heard right: the mods were back! This was mostly the fault of the Jam, a sort-of punk band who sought to differentiate themselves from their safety-pin-bothering competitors by wearing mod-inspired get-ups and publicly acknowledging their musical debt to the Who and the

Small Faces. It isn't hard to see why mod, with its indisputably working-class credentials and insistence on straight trouser legs, would be more attractive to a generation of sort-of punks than any other dead youth cult you care to name. But it must have been tough, in those early days, to know just how to go about setting yourself up as a nu-mod – you could look to the Jam's Paul Weller for fashion tips, but how would you know how to talk, how to dance, what you were supposed to stand for? Enter *Quadrophenia*. A hundred and fifteen minutes alone in a cinema with *that* thing and *any* idiot could work out what they were supposed to do: talk like Phil Daniels, dance like Sting and *worship* The Who.

The film quickly became a sacred text to the nu-mods, and Little East Street – the tiny alley in which Phil Daniels' character, Jimmy, brusquely shags Steph (Leslie Ash) – became a pilgrimage site.[5] Then there was that long, bulky green parka Jimmy wore in the film – you needed to have one, and wear it literally all the time, or you weren't a 'proper' mod (the fact that the original mods only really wore parkas to protect their posh threads when the weather was bad didn't enter into it). Consequently, any gathering of nu-mods – like the ones you used to see in Churchill Square on Saturday afternoons, as late in the day as 1986 – tended to resemble a handful of burst damsons scattered on the breeze; a less intimidating effect could hardly be imagined.

They were, for the most part, scooterless, and the parkas made it impossible to tell how nice their suits were, but they shouted 'we are we are we are the mods' a lot so you could still just about tell who they were supposed to be. My sister hung around with them for a spell, and they generally seemed like normal, friendly, mild-mannered people who just happened to have loads of really

---

[5] Even today its walls are plastered with emotional tributes from the faithful (LANCING MODS 4 EVA, JIMMY WE DID IT HERE FOR YOU LUV CRAIG + SAZ), although the back yard in which the epoch-making boff actually took place is now overlooked by the kitchens of Momma Cherri's Soul Food Shack, so anyone still keen to re-enact it had better be prepared to end up smelling like gumbo.

cool old records. But this air of inherent amiability only added to the impression that they were a kind of youth-cultural Amish, stolidly refusing to acknowledge anything that happened to the rest of the world after a certain point in history – 1966, in their case (with a special dispensation for Weller). This seemed a shame, not only because it meant they could never listen to any Prince (who I was very big on at the time), but also because it was precisely the sort of attitude the original mods they so admired would have scorned. Those early mods had loved *pop* – frequently obscure American pop, but pop nonetheless; they derided the rockers on the basis that their musical taste and dress code were locked in a 1950s' time warp. It could, then, be argued that whenever they ogled the Italian tailoring in *Quadrophenia* or sneered to see a schoolmate buy a Duran Duran record, the nu-mods were actually behaving a lot more like . . . old rockers.

In any case, they soldiered on – ditching the parkas (or at least getting nicer-looking ones, with proper hoods and that), surviving a lengthy and convoluted internecine struggle against the mod-yet-anti-mod 'scooterists'[6] and even briefly regaining near-prominence during the mid-1990s 'Britpop' fad. Back in 1986 you wouldn't have bet on them seeing out the winter, but in spite of their occasionally confused approach they were still the nearest thing to a proper youth cult around at the time.

There were punks, of course, but a lot of those who'd eschewed goth were now starting to metamorphose into 'crusties': black leather and gobbing were out, German army surplus shirts and vegan anarcho-syndicalism were in. Bands like Crass and Chumbawamba were among the first to politicise the punks, but it was the Levellers – formed in Brighton in 1988 – who became the first real crustie standard bearers. The incorporation of folk

---

[6] This particularly ludicrous example of sub-cultural in-fighting would no doubt warrant a whole book – or at least a thought-provoking, bittersweet Radio 4 play – all to itself, but it's like the Time War in *Doctor Who*: you often hear people mention it but always in a measured, cryptic way, as though possession of the full facts would be enough to send a mortal mind mad.

music elements into their songs was either an attempt to connect with Britain's long secret history of dissent or an excuse for self-righteous hectoring, depending on your point of view, but there was no denying their commitment. In 1994 they bought the old Metway factory near Queen's Park and converted it into a studio where a day's time every week is given free to an up-and-coming Brighton band; critical darlings British Sea Power and Clearlake both recorded early demos there. It's also worth noting that their song 'One Way' (*There's only one way of life/ And that's your own*) became an anthem for travellers and other alternative lifestylers everywhere, although the sentiment always seemed a bit off to me: what if you were living the life of a homicidal maniac or, indeed, that of a squatter-starving capitalist pig?

As their name unwittingly suggests, a lot of the crusties were really quite *old*. Perhaps it was the fiddles, perhaps it was the fleas, but for one reason or another The Kids – especially the working-class ones – tended to stay away. Which was just as well, really, because something a lot more entertaining was already starting to happen elsewhere.

House music first hit the British charts in late 1986 with the release of Farley 'Jackmaster' Funk's 'Love Can't Turn Around'. Essentially an evolution of disco, but with a sparer sound and the capacity to take advantage of the innovations in music technology that had driven pop throughout the early 1980s, house had emerged from the gay club scenes of Chicago and New York but achieved its first mainstream success in Britain. To the uninitiated, perhaps even balding *Top of the Pops* viewer, its early hits sounded bewilderingly simplistic – all you had to do, it seemed, was sit on a drum machine and say 'jack' a lot – but the girls (and, of course, gays) in the clubs understood.

The genre developed at an astonishingly rapid pace, splintering almost instantaneously into dozens of discrete but notoriously hard-to-pin-down sub-genres; of these, 'acid house' was perhaps the least obviously commercial. Its driving force was the Roland

303 bass synthesiser, which makes a bizarre but unmistakable noise that cannot accurately be described by any other word but 'squelchy'. Anyone hearing that noise for the first time might well think you'd have to be off your head to like it – this was, of course, true.

Those in the know around London's clubland had already been necking the occasional Ecstasy pill – another American import – for several years, but the drug didn't become widely available in Britain until 1987/88, just as house was beginning to dominate British pop music. The pill and the squelch went together like bacon and eggs, but nightclub security staff could not always be relied upon to understand this. Worse still, even cutting-edge venues like Brighton's Zap Club were forced to close long before daybreak because of the licensing laws – a truly intolerable situation for anyone who'd just done their third 'disco biscuit'. The logical solution, much to the chagrin of unwary farmers through-out the catchment area of the M25 and the delight of budding DJs throughout the excellently-placed-in-this-regard town of Brighton, was to take it outside.

The popular press got all over the 'rave' scene at the earliest opportunity and asked someone or other (not specified) to Stop This Sick Filth That Poisons Our Kids, thereby convincing any kids as yet untouched by said Filth that they should get hold of some but fast. The *cri de coeur* of the johnny-come-latelies was provided by D-Mob's hit 'We Call It Acid' – to wit, 'ACIIIEEEED!!'; a lot of them actually were on acid, which wasn't supposed to be the point at all. Contemptuous of this, and unwilling to share dancefloor/pasture space with the sort of people who used to beat them up at school, the squintingly elitist middle-class clubbers who'd been the first to embrace acid house moved on to other things: 'intelligent jungle', 'progressive trance', 'dark gabba' ... whatever. But it didn't really matter what the flava-of-the-month was because the free party infrastructure was now firmly in place, and raves of one sort or another would continue to occur ad infinitum.

As for Brighton, well, the whole thing was right up our alley. Most importantly, we had a large crustie population who were more than willing to view the illegal party culture as yet another all-out assault on that busybody Man's interfering ways (nothing to do with the fact that it gave them a chance to finally enjoy the kind of blank-brained euphoria job-holding ravers had been enjoying in the clubs, I'm *sure*). Links were duly formed with the university-leaving milksop fraternity who then, as now, dictated the musical contents of 'the underground', and between them they managed to organise a viable alternative to the pastoral rave: the ravey squat party.

Partying in Brighton itself was obviously a lot more convenient for everybody – no more damp ankles, no more poorly signposted B roads and, best of all, no more mithering from the crusties about the shameful levels of carbon emission involved in giving them a lift out of town. The first ravey squat parties (or, if I might make so bold, 'disco squats') I ever heard of were held, both nights of every weekend, in an abandoned shop next door to the Sainsbury's on London Road. When that fell through they went over to the competition, moving directly across the street to the cavernous spaces above Somerfield; by this time the various DJ collectives were so well organised that the Somerfield parties resembled proper nightclubs in all but health and safety legislation, with professional sound systems and lighting rigs and even someone taking (voluntarily donated) money at the door. Unfortunately, the passing of the Criminal Justice and Public Order Act in 1994[7] put paid to any such clearly visible shape-throwing,

---

[7] The Act gave police new powers to stop any party where loud music was deemed to be causing a nuisance; ' "music" ', it clarified, 'includes sounds wholly or predominantly characterised by the emission of a succession of repetitive beats.' Many of those opposed to the Act at the time grew very fond of poking fun at this phrase, and electro pioneers Autechre painstakingly constructed a track called 'Flutter' which contained no repeated beats of any kind, in the hope that it would therefore be immune from police action. They'd overlooked that word 'includes', though, so had no way of knowing it was a total waste of time.

and the collectives had to seek a less conspicuous venue. Opting for a disused storage pen at Shoreham Power Station was a shrewd move – even the police couldn't be arsed going to Shoreham most of the time.

Despite loving both free things and parties, I was never much of a fixture on the free party circuit. Often this was because hearing the bell for last orders made me think happy thoughts of home, to the extent where any suggestion that, instead of just going there, I should squeeze into an overcrowded Mini belonging to someone called 'Hellish' and be driven to a condemned cement works many miles away with no guarantee of return seemed almost offensively inappropriate. I did manage to go to a couple of those supermarket do's but somehow my innate prissiness always got in the way of my enjoyment. *We're not supposed to be here,* I'd fret defiantly through the merry haze of my drug intake. *When you do something you're not supposed to, bad things happen. Overdoses, murders, rapes, stabbings ... And the whole building could just collapse on our heads at any moment!!* The fact that there was often a policeman or two on the door to keep an eye on things[8] only made matters worse: *But this is supposed to be illegal! They must have taken a back-hander from the party organisers ... That means they'll turn a blind eye to anything bad that happens! Oh dear God, we're DOOMED!*

The music didn't help. Crusties generally favoured the aggressively dehumanised pounding of 'hard trance' over the more upbeat, vocal-based tracks then doing the rounds of the gay clubs, and for people like me who enjoyed upbeat, vocal-based music but were ridiculously afraid of going to any one gay club more than once a year this was beginning to feel like a problem. The problem wasn't unique to Brighton – clubbers and ravers everywhere were reporting a growing sense of dissatisfaction with the anally retentive, trainspotterish tendencies of their DJs, who seemed more interested in playing endless games of cooler-than-

---

[8] I know! You could even ask them for directions in those days.

thou oneupmanship with their rivals than playing records that would actually cause people to have *fun* – but its solution, for once, was. Big Beat!

In 1996, promoter Gareth Hansome teamed up with Damien Harris, owner of Brighton-based independent record label Skint, to launch the Big Beat Boutique club night at the Concorde (like the Florida Rooms, a rather down-at-heel bar in the Aquarium Terraces). The night was conceived as a showcase for Skint's output, and its house style emerged seemingly by dint of a mutual agreement that there should be *no* house style; the result, in the words of one devotee, was 'Fat chunky basslines mixed with old sixties samples, funky disco riffs, blasts of guitar and hip-hop breaks'[9] – in short, anything that seemed to make the punters smile. One DJ in particular began to flourish in this novel environment, and in so doing surprised everyone. He was, after all, virtually your dad's age, and had only fetched up at the Boutique on account of being Gareth Hansome's flatmate.

It would be impossible to invent a more stereotypically Brightonesque career in the music industry than the one Norman Cook had been enjoying – on and off – up to this point. Born in Reigate, he moved to Brighton to study at the Polytechnic but was subsequently lured to Hull by a friend with a band whose bass player had left them in the lurch. He joined the band (the Housemartins), which went on to have two hit singles but split up shortly afterwards (in the first, but not the last, Cook-related incidence of 'the Piranha effect'). He returned to Brighton in 1988 and formed Beats International, who had a massive hit with *Dub Be Good To Me* but were immediately sued over it (having 'sampled' the bassline from the Clash's *Guns of Brixton*), and split up shortly after the release of their poorly received second album. Undaunted, Cook put together an acid jazz-funk combo – Freak Power – who had a hit with a song that had been on a jeans advert. After they'd failed to follow up this early success he

[9] 'Lola Cherry', talking to the *Evening Argus*.

became besotted with house music, and recorded an album of it under the handle 'Pizzaman' in 1995; one of the tunes, 'Happiness', became a hit and got used on a fruit juice advert.

No matter how much anyone liked Norm – and most people in Brighton always seemed to, if perhaps a little more in his troughs than his peaks – it was hard to avoid the conclusion that a pattern was forming. He was that rarest of pop stars (by my reckoning, the only other British example would be *Jonathan King!*): a serial one-hit wonder. If he'd just released all his records under the name 'Norman Cook's Current Thing' he'd already have had enough to flog a Greatest Hits off the back of, but because he'd had the decency to keep his various endeavours conceptually discrete he was unfairly perceived as a four-or-more-times loser.

In this way he came to embody everything that was great and yet a bit crap about aspiring musicians in Brighton past, present and future. We all know the form: you go to a pub on Friday night and drunkenly agree to provide the soundtrack for someone's experimental CGI film, wake up the next afternoon and realise you've lost the bloke's number, go to another pub and meet some goths who need a bassist for a few weeks, join them and tour Austria for a month supporting Marianne Faithfull (who fails to personally acknowledge you even when you're carrying her hat box), get officially sworn in as a permanent member of the band because your 'shit' is 'darker' than that of their real bass player, fall out with them over a restaurant bill and leave the band two days later, stop back in at the first pub you went to and run into that CGI bloke again (he's forgotten all about the film, though), shake your head in disbelief as you learn that his girlfriend was actually the goths' original bassist, agree that the three of you should get an acid jazz-funk combo together (just to see the looks on their faces!) and so very *on* . . .

Any true Brighton muso will always have at least half a dozen failed 'projects' under their belt, all of which they will gladly discuss in tones of astonishing solemnity, occasionally flattering you with the implication that of *course* you can see there's something missing from modern music before bashfully admitting that their last project probably *would have been that thing* – if only someone hadn't stole the idea/ the Criminal Justice Act hadn't come in/ 'Hellish' hadn't gone off to do a TEFL[10] course. Brighton DJs can't really do this, of course (a DJ's 'project' is, by its nature, singular and ongoing), so they generally just slag off Norman Cook instead.

Cook performed at the Boutique as Fatboy Slim, a glib pseudonym which nonetheless conformed to Seymour Skinner of *The Simpsons*' definition of a classic band name – 'a name that's witty at first, but that seems less funny each time you hear it'. His reputation for providing good nights out had soon grown to a point where even posh London folk were taking an interest – not least indie/dance crossover hotshots the Chemical Brothers, who personally encouraged 'Fatboy' to start making records of his own (using bits of other people's). His cheaply recorded first album, *Better Living Through Chemistry*, won critical acclaim and modest commercial success, and gave Cook the confidence and clout to take an altogether slicker approach on the follow-up *You've Come a Long Way, Baby*. The first anyone heard of this was the single 'Rockafeller Skank', a freakishly invigorating blend of manic breakbeats, twangy surf guitar and standard issue hip-hop MC gibberish quite unlike anything we'd heard before (although cynics detected a spiritual debt to Jive Bunny). Joyously stupid and as catchy as you like, it hit big not just here but all over the world; they used it in *hundreds* of adverts.

Brighton's hipsters were, at first, delighted – good old Norm with his novelty records! – but when his next two singles repeated the success their attitude grew frostier. Twenty years earlier they'd probably have accused him of 'selling out', but since that phrase

---

[10] That's 'Teaching English as a Foreign Language'. Every crustie in Brighton not currently touring with the Levellers is doing, or thinking of doing, a TEFL course; they'd have you believe it's a global outreach matter, but sadly it's just a cowardly escape plan for when the sea levels rise and Britain becomes the new Atlantis.

had by now been expunged from the pop-cultural lexicon they had to content themselves with grumbling about gimmickry and insisting he'd always been the worst DJ at the Boutique anyway. At a time when they might have been expected to feel proud of their town they behaved more as though their pride had been wounded – which, in a way, it had. The Brighton they'd been proud of was a place where everyone was hugely talented but 'got something together' only on very rare occasions and with no expectations of mainstream popularity (because no one outside Brighton could possibly be trusted to understand it). In shucking off his one-hit-wonder status Cook had inadvertently exposed this other Brighton as an agoraphobic delusion, and no one who'd chosen to settle down there would be thanking him for it any time soon.

By this time the Concorde had been demolished and the Big Beat Boutique night moved to a flashy, trashy tourist trap that had recently opened on the seafront called The Beach, prompting many of its earliest and most passionate followers to declare it officially and irretrievably Over. But in the rest of the world, where they've always been slower to catch on to these things, people were only just starting to get excited about the new style of music it had spawned. A friend of mine visiting New York at around this time was amazed to find an immense collage of Big Beat Boutique ephemera completely covering the back wall of Liquid City, a record shop so painfully hip he'd half-expected to be ridiculed for his comparative ignorance of obscure Detroit techno the moment he walked through the door. Noticing his accent, a shop assistant made the usual American mistake of asking if he was Australian. When he replied that he was actually from Brighton, England, her jaw fell open. 'You're joking, right?' she asked, as if incredulous that anyone who actually *came* from Brighton would want to do anything but stay there. 'My God! So what's it *really like?*'

I know – that sounds totally made up. But it's *true*, I swear to God! And the most shocking part of the whole story is that when he came back and told me what had happened I felt, for several minutes, like jumping madly up and down, even though we were on the bus to work at the time. After so many years of watching Brighton's thriving live music network produce nothing but runners-up and also-rans (however lovable), it felt weirdly *liberating* to finally see one of our own reach the big leagues with a type of music that had (arguably) been born here: *we'd* always known we were the coolest but now, at last, everyone else was going to have to face it too.

Little did I know that the architects of this unusual sensation were already entertaining doubts of their own. Looking back on those times for a special report about the Boutique's sixth anniversary in 2002, Damien Harris told the *Argus*: 'We had to deal with Norman's success and we suffered slightly from the tourist syndrome. For a while we were media darlings, everyone was writing about us and I don't think Brighton had ever had anything like that before. We had coined a name for this music which we have been trying to get away from ever since.' In other words, 'Everyone was getting really excited, people were coming in from out of town just to see us and we made tons of money . . . Didn't like it.' And why not? Because that sort of thing is *so not Brighton*! Apparently the Boutique crew had rediscovered their Brighton hipster roots at the last minute and remembered that 'mainstream' should be viewed as the exact opposite of 'cool'. As for making a *fuss* about anything – how uncool is that? Cook himself picked up the thread – 'Everyone else started playing big beat and we switched back to house, just to be awkward' – before expanding on a few of the more personal agonies inflicted upon him by the cruel hand of mass public validation: 'It got to a point where everybody was expecting me to pogo up and down and perform, waving my hands in the air . . . I was like a caricature of myself.' I don't know about you, but I still expect him to do that myself – probably because he does, in fact, still do it.

But fun is a hard thing to turn your back on, whether you're a superstar DJ or an embittered player-hater. For all his big talk about getting sick of us, and ours about getting sick of him, we all knew, deep down, that we'd shared something special which deserved another chance. That's why, on 7 July 2001, Norman Cook was to be found on a specially constructed stage on Brighton beach, playing a set almost entirely composed of Big Beat favourites and making a caricature of himself all over again in front of 35,000 people.

The event – Big 'Beach' Boutique, ho ho – went down a storm; it was as if we'd never even rowed. Part of its success was attributable to timing, inasmuch as the backlash against big beat now seemed almost as distant as its glory days, and for the hipsters who'd been piling on the scorn the whole thing was just far enough in the past that when they heard, say, Norman's stormin' remix of Cornershop's 'Brimful of Asha', they felt free to shout 'Hey, it's *this*!' on the basis that it was now practically 'retro'. Video footage of the occasion shows a whole beachload of people seemingly in the grip of the very feeling I got on the bus that time – top o' the world, Ma! – and no one appears to be enjoying it more than the man himself. As he holds up a piece of card urging the crowd to 'wave to the boats', his ecstatic grin covers so much of his face that it almost warrants a thought bubble of its own – 'we must do this again sometime', perhaps.

The second Big Beach Boutique event was held on 13 July 2002. It was an extremely hot day, the kind that makes Londoners long for a bit more sky to look at; extensive press promotion and a rumoured flyer campaign at Victoria Station encouraged around two hundred thousand of them to come down here for a bit of ours. By an unsettlingly ironic coincidence my enchanting collaboratrix and I were staying overnight in London at the time, but from what I've heard it all got a bit hectic. Around teatime, I mean – after that it was just bloody ridiculous.

One thing I've never really understood about parties: if no one turns up it's clearly a rubbish party, if loads of people do it's clearly a great one, but what if *so many* people come that you can't dance or get a second drink or even see anything apart from the back-print on the man in front of you's T-shirt? Would that, according to traditional party logic, be *the best party ever*? If so, then yes – we had the best party ever, right here on Brighton beach. But for the family of the woman who died, or the many emergency workers who had stress-related nervous breakdowns as a direct result, or even the hundreds of Londoners who had to sleep in their own filth on the beach that night (see how inclusive I can be?), it probably wasn't one for the photo album.

Unfortunately for the *Argus* and, to a lesser extent, me, no one was strictly to blame. The Londoners weren't – because what is this town *for*, if not to remind jaded Londoners what it means to be alive (providing you pack 'em back on to the train Sunday night)?[11] Norm wasn't, because he'd already raised concerns about the show's potential for mayhem with the council ('I've been told the beach has a capacity of 125,000. I find that hard to believe because there were only 35,000 last year and I couldn't see a single square metre of beach. But the council doesn't seem concerned'). So can we blame the council? I'd like to – you *know* I would! – but you'd have to have as much faith in their street-smarts as they do themselves to seriously believe they could have known how many 'kidz' would consider Fatboy 'da bomb'.

At the end of the day it was just one of those weird things – not unlike the mod/ rocker clashes of '64 – that occasionally happen here as a result of our unique relationship with London. For more than two hundred years the capital's citizenry have looked on Brighton as a kind of informal pleasure-bank, to be spontaneously popped into whenever the mood takes them, and for the most part this has served us all well. As with any bank, though, we've only been able to operate as such on the understanding that our customers won't all try to make a withdrawal at once; when that happens, as it clearly did on 13 July 2002, they have to be sent away empty-handed and the whole fragile edifice of our brand-identity crumbles to the ground. It

---

[11] I myself have often visited Torquay for the same reason.

probably won't ever happen the same way again, because Brighton's increasing resemblance to London makes it unlikely that such a quintessentially Brightonesque pop sensation could ever again be possible, but if, by some mad fluke, we ever do manage to whip something up, they *will* be back. Perhaps those agoraphobic hipsters had a point, then, and we should just keep the good stuff to ourselves in future ... ? That certainly seems to be the thinking behind 2007's Big Beach show, for which only people with a BN postcode are eligible to buy tickets, but this eminently sensible precaution is bound to lead to a creeping sense of anticlimax on the night. Add to that the fact that it will not actually be held on the beach but on a closed-off Madeira Drive and it begins to look a lot like the backward provincial cousin of its more charismatic predecessors; like a Radio 1 Roadshow, in fact, but without the 'goodie bags'.

Oh, but why should *I* gripe? I'm practically – perhaps even literally – middle-aged now, so it really isn't any of my business. This sad fact was finally brought home to me a couple of years ago, at the last illegal party I will ever go to, just outside Ovingdean. It was actually a very good venue for a party: on the beach and close to a main road, but set well apart from the rest of civilisation by a dizzyingly high chalk cliff with a stone stairway running down it. It wasn't a very good party, though. Imagine the central tableau of Bosch's *Garden of Earthly Delights* restaged in modern dress and near-darkness with a few extra gallons of puke and urine thrown in and you *still* won't be further than halfway towards getting an accurate mental picture of that monstrous jumble: thousands of people, all pissed up or on drugs, with the overwhelming majority wanting desperately to get from the middle to the edge of the throng but destined to forget why and turn back as soon as they got there. The music was terrifyingly loud near the speakers but not quite loud enough everywhere else, so whenever anyone shouted something incoherent in your ear about needing to get some pills or needing to get rid of some or looking for their dog or the sea – which they all did, all the time – there was no way you could reasonably ignore them. No one was actually dancing.

I made the best of it, of course (you do, don't you?), and spent a fairly agreeable couple of hours staring at the sea and humming tunelessly to myself. With honour thus satisfied I set about trying to get a lift home, but none of my associates would hear of it. 'The sun'll be coming up soon, Dan,' they peevishly observed. 'We've *got* to stay for that.'

We did. It was not, however, the glorious, many-hued, cathartically awe-inspiring sunrise I'd foolishly allowed myself to anticipate but something more like the grudging roll of a grubby dimmer switch. The sun itself was completely hidden behind a wall of cloud, so its presence could only be discerned by the stealthy incursion of light and colour into the party and its surroundings; every subtle shift in its intensity revealed a little more in the way of fag ends, half-eaten burgers, broken bottles, dog (hopefully) turds, used condoms and broken syringes, and made everyone's eyes look just that little bit madder. I felt as though the whole fabric of reality was deteriorating in direct proportion to my state of mind: it was the most hideously *pertinent* comedown I've ever been through.

I vowed never to return, and this was just as well because, not too many weekends later, a yardie crime gang from London descended on Ovingdean, stationed an armed guard at the top of the stone stairway to charge 'admission' and let it be known that they'd be quite badly cheesed off if anyone other than them tried to sell any drugs. (People kind of stopped going after that.) These days I seldom make it any further than the pub at the end of the road, and while this has led to an overall improvement in my quality of life it also means I cannot even begin to speculate as to what's currently going down in Brighton's teen haunts. My sources inform me that dance music is less popular than it used to be, with a lot more clubs devoting nights to guitar-based indie and metal music (they do still say 'indie', don't they?). In terms of bands, our hottest prospects are the aforementioned British Sea Power and

Clearlake, both of whom are quite good but never seem to get on the radio, and the misleadingly monikered Kooks, who aren't but do. There's also the Go Team, who make exhilarating, sample-laden dance music not a million miles away from the supposedly forbidden rhythms of Big Beat (somebody tell Norman!). Sadly, however, the only band with significant Brighton connections to really make its mark on the charts in recent years is Nizlopi, whose execrable 'JCB Song' became the Christmas number two in 2005. It was a profoundly embarrassing time – although Nizlopi aren't Brighton born and bred, the unmistakeable whiff of mouldy-flapjack 'authenticity' which permeates that record betrayed how much time they'd been spending with our musos – but, fingers crossed, it now appears that their hit-making career got thrown away with the paper crowns and silly string residue.

Youth cults still exist but there seems to be more overlap between them than previously, and some don't even have proper names(!). I'm in two minds about this: it can't be bad that today's teenagers are more open-minded about music and, to some extent, less insecure about their identities than their forebears were, but aren't they also missing out on something? No one who was a mod or rocker in the 60s will ever forget the idiotic thrill of waging desultory war against an easily identifiable cross-section of their peers, and no punk ever felt more like a punk than when a bunch of schoolkids shouted, 'Oi, punk!' at them and then ran away as soon as they turned around. In the olden days, experiences like these enabled you to cope with the horror of adolescence by clearly defining it as a frantic and foolish time; deep down you always knew you wouldn't, *couldn't* carry on like that indefinitely, and this helped reassure you that the zits and the nerves and the angst would prove similarly short-lived. Not only that, it frightened teachers and made your mum cross. Kids, I'm telling you – you *need* to do this, before it's too late! Just don't do it anywhere near where I live.

Also, please don't come and get me. This is actually the key point of my whole thesis, and as such cannot be overstated. Every time I've been in town since I started writing this chapter I've spotted a mod – usually ageing, but often surprisingly brawny – and where I would normally have thought, 'Aww, innit sweet?', I now feel my heart being pierced by an icy dart of fear. Will they ever get back to him, the things I said? Will he one day look at me and think, 'There's that wanker who had a go at mods'? Will he come and get me? And that old punk, over there – you can tell just by looking that he's been dressing like that since '77. Will he one day look at me and think 'The Depressions were *way* more important to the Brighton punk scene than the Lillettes – that wanker just didn't mention them because they don't have a funny name!'? Will he, too, come and get me? Probably not. But will he write me a boring letter?

Even after I've got home I find it hard to put these concerns completely out of my mind. And even if I get completely out of my mind before I turn in it's impossible to sleep without dreaming, *dreaming* ... I see myself running faster than I've ever run, pelting up the beach opposite the Odeon and into the subway; at first it looks like I'm just doing it for the good of my health (that's probably the weirdest bit), but when I round the corner and start up the ramp to West Street they start coming in after me. Heavy boots smack the concrete – a great many heavy boots. I'm halfway to the Clock Tower before I dare to look around, and the moment I do I wish I hadn't. It's them all right, but who'd have thought there'd be so *many*? Mods, punks, ravers and crusties make up the vanguard, while skaters, emo kids, people who like 'krunk' and all the others I didn't even have the courtesy to mention bring up the rear. Every one of them is wielding a piece of broken deckchair as though it's a club.

I make it past the Clock Tower but end up going to ground in that graveyard behind Pizza Hut, lungs burning as I wheeze and sob. Sensing my surrender they approach slowly, almost casually, and begin to surround me. So many angry faces: Norman Cook suddenly looks more like Norman Tebbit, Jimmy out of *Quadro-phenia* seems to have forgotten he's really Phil Daniels and – oh, dear God – even *Cliff*'s got murder in his eyes! 'Congratulations,' he sneers, raising the club as high as he can over his head. Seeing this, the mob of youth cultists surges forward with a cheer, nearly toppling him; I take advantage of the ensuing confusion to stand up and make one last desperate stab at diverting them.

'Guys – *guys*,' I wheedle. 'You all want to get me, and you probably think it's going to feel pretty great when you finally do, but just take a look around you: hasn't something great happened *already*? You've spent all these years fighting amongst yourselves, but today, for the first time, you've been working together – mod with rocker, punk with ted, goth with human! And if there's just one person among you who's changed their minds about getting me then you should just call this whole thing off, because when the kids are united they can never be –'

(BOP!)

PUTTING THE SEX IN SUSSEX

In the October of 2006, a most curious headline appeared in Brighton's fun-packed local paper, the *Argus*. FATHER FIGHTS STRIP CLUB IN 'FAMILY AREA' it read – and I was pleasantly surprised to see that this normally not over-worldly publication had seen fit to put those inverted commas in. For while East Street is not as wild as West Street – 'Little Beirut' as the police have been known to call it – it is certainly something of a haunt for pleasure-seekers after dark, albeit those on a bigger budget. An upmarket, partly pedestrianised shopping street crammed with bars and restaurants – think South Molton Street with the appealing additions of the screech of seagulls, and that little alley where Jimmy the mod fucked his sallow dream-girl Steph in *Quadrophenia*. It's Burberry Prorsum to West Street's Burberry proper, but it needn't get too far up its own fundament; if someone goes there after eight on a weekend night, chances are they got themselves dressed with a definite view to getting themselves undressed by somebody else.

Which is what made it a bit odd that a resident should have called it 'an inappropriate location' for a fully nude lap-dancing club. A bit like saying Duke's Mound was a daft place for gays to go cruising, or that anyone looking to get drunk up West Street on a Saturday night was basically on a fool's errand. But the father of three cast his net of lunacy even wider when he followed the local objection up with: 'More broadly I object on moral grounds. *Brighton is not the sort of city where we want establishments of this type.*' (My incredulous italics.)

On the contrary, Brighton has been synonymous with sex since Prinnie shacked up here with Mrs Fitzherbert, and the smut-fest by the sea can be seen in everything from saucy postcards bearing legends like 'Ooo, will I really sink if you take your finger out, Mr Badcock?' to salacious phone cards suggesting 'blow your mind with my behind'. In 1922 – with typically amockalyptic, sex-starved ill-humour – T.S. Eliot used the phrase 'a weekend at the Metropole' as a metaphor for moral decline in 'The Wasteland'; as this was the place where I took my husband's virginity one weekend more than a decade ago, I resent this personally as well as finding it philosophically a bit suspect. In 1979 the first ever British nudist beach was established here; its main advocate was, rather charmingly and eccentrically, the Tory councillor and grandmother Eileen Jakes, who believed that the 200-yard stretch of shingle would radically increase tourism. So it seems odd that citizens are throwing up their hands about attractive women getting their kit off in the relative seclusion of a lap-dancing club when unattractive men have been doing the same in broad daylight for a quarter of a century.

This is a sexy city, no two ways – Ooo, missus! – about it. As John Osborne said in a rare moment of approval, 'I never had lunch in Brighton without wanting to take a woman to bed in the afternoon . . . to shudder one's last, thrusting, replete gasp between the sheets at 4 and 6 o'clock in Brighton would be the most perfect last earthly delight.'

It might have been him who said – but don't quote me on this – 'You can smell the sperm in the air.' And, of course, the amyl nitrate. But recently, you can smell the baby-sick too. And this Invasion of the Bourgeois Breeders – see the Fuming Father of East Street – is causing the sort of social discomfort and public disorder that the bush-whackers and butt-pluggers of Kemp Town never did.

You can't blame the Breeders, logically speaking, for coming here; London sucks, and Brighton rocks. If you have young children and live in the capital, imagine how tempting the thought of moving here must appear; between downs and sea they'll flourish, while you make the daily 50-minute hop to the Smoke and back. Yet somehow, when relocating from your particular plot of the capital's Nappy Valley, you were so busy wiping little India's nose and asking Harry repeatedly if he wanted to 'pee' that you failed to notice the bootylicious boys bending, blowing and buggering each other on every street corner. You were so high on the smell of sea, sushi and Fairtrade coffee that you failed to get a whiff of the sperm of which John Osborne, or someone like him, spoke. So when your little darling skidded one sunny morning on a used condom on the way to Tumbletots, it came as something of a shock to realise that you were living the modern sexual paradox of B&H. Namely, that half the incomers came here to pursue sexual excess, and the other half to escape the sexual excesses of London. In short, the in-laws versus the outlaws.

They don't half take up some space, too, the breeders. It's not just Brightonians who notice it; in November 2006 the *London Standard*'s Charlotte Ross wrote:

> If you ever wondered where old clubbers go to chill out, I now know the answer. Brighton is teeming with them, and they are multiplying like mad. The lively south coast has become a giant crèche for burnt-out

Londoners. During a recent visit I found it hard to locate a single adult who wasn't actively parenting, heavily pregnant or discussing the subject loudly in the street. A stroll through the town centre, with tired mums letting feral infants run amok, and traffic jams of giant buggies, was a modern-day assault course. Upper Street on Saturday seems positively tranquil by contrast.

When Brighton scores higher than Islington on the double buggy count, you know there's something amiss in Sin City. Even people who had moved here with a view to nesting began to find the place too kiddified for their liking, such as the young professional pregnant woman who wrote to me that she had moved here from London believing that it was a good place to bring up a family, only to find herself so repelled by our 'vacuous, affluent Toytown' that she promptly hot-footed it to Southampton, 'which feels like a real city, and where three-wheeler buggies are rare'.

They do take up a lot of space, the incoming Bourgeois Breeders and their monster cars and their mega buggies and their massive self-regard. They wheel into you at Pride, presuming right of way simply for the fact of having spawned, and a couple of days later they complain that there were a few blowjobs going on in the bushes. Maybe I'm missing the point here, but why go to a gay day out and then be surprised that there's a bit of the actual thing that people define themselves as being gay because of going on? Blaming gays for giving each other blowjobs is like blaming breeders for breeding or dogs for barking. And it's not as if they're such shrinking violets when it comes to bodily functions themselves. Queuing for a surreal happening outside of a mobile maze during the 2006 Brighton Fringe Festival, my husband and I were unlucky enough to be standing behind your archetype Bo-Brees, who repeatedly interrogated their small daughter thus: 'Rivka, do you want to do a pee? Do you? *Do you? Do you want to do a pee?!*' There were many reasons why I bitterly resented this scenario. Firstly, it was a beautiful day and we were trying to appreciate it serenely without issues of infantile water-passing being harped on repeatedly. Secondly, Rivka had no right to have an Icelandic name and yet use the taxpayers' facilities, the way I look at it. Thirdly, the parents who ceaselessly raised this profoundly private issue had voices of such loud-hailer middle-class boastfulness – so absolutely sure that every syllable they spoke was fascinating to the rest of the people trying to appreciate that lovely summer day in their own way – that they seemed to be actually undertaking some undefined 'parenting test', for the benefit of some unseen eye, with their utterances – and to heck with us innocent bystanders.

One could only imagine how these types might decry 'chav' parents and their legendary loudness in public places. Speaking of which, when did you last hear the fabled supermarket cry of the harassed prole mum as she slaps her wailing tot around the legs: '*Now* you've got something to cry about!' As parental callousness goes, I was extremely alarmed that day to note that Rivka's parents, being fully aware of the unreliable state of her bladder, nevertheless marched her into the Maze of Grotesqueries, where obviously the floodgates could have been opened by any number of random horrors – and those who trod after her on the weary path to bizarre enlightenment could obviously take their chances when it came to what they stepped in. As if to drive home the fact that Brighton breeders are far more eager than Brighton benders to flaunt their sexual organs, we had not made our way halfway through this little sideshow of horrors when we stumbled upon a trio of blatantly breastfeeding women, sitting on the ground and grinning at all comers for all the world like a lactating girl-group. Except with tits no one, not anyone in the world or in prison or anywhere, wanted them to get out. Ever.

The last man to be hanged for buggery in Brighton met his end in 1835, and ever since then it's pretty much been Liberty-Hall-on-Sea down here. The combination of the railway link of 1841, day-trippers – including many fags of convenience – finally getting a chance to do things they wouldn't do on their own London doorstep and an already louche atmosphere made it a pleasure destination as much as a leisure resort.

Mind you, even hanging had never really put them off. The stationing of a huge number of soldiers here during the Napoleonic Wars acted as a total gay-magnet, though, then as now, loving a man in uniform was not always recip- rocated and in August 1822, George Wilson, a servant from Newcastle upon Tyne, was accused by a guardsman he had met in the Duke of Wellington public house in Pool Valley of having offered him a sovereign and two shillings to go with him on to the beach to commit an unnatural crime. But even the abolition of taking it up the wrong 'un as a capital crime did not always lead to a happy ending; in May 1836, Stanley Stokes, a London solicitor who had been making sexual approaches to a groom at the New Ship Hotel, was mobbed and tarred and cut his own throat in East Street, dying two days later.

Lesbians were as ever less flagrant and thus public; it's no mere oversight that they've never caught Ellen de Generes, Rosie O'Donnell – or even me, heh heh! – looking for love in a public convenience. It was more a case of by-their- nesting-shall-you-know-them when it came to chicks; who had time for hot toilet sex when there were curtains to be chosen, or to munch a rug when there were rugs to be laid! In the past a pair of spinsters could set up house together and people would simply think it was a no-sex-please-we'reskittish type of thing – as opposed to these sex-soaked days when one only has to be seen talking to a man, woman or dog in the street for everyone to assume that one is at least on heavy-petting terms with him/her/it. Thus the philanthropist Angela Burdett-Coutts, who died (presumably with a smile on her face) in 1906, spent part of each year on holiday at the Royal Albion Hotel in Brighton with her companion, Hannah. The couple were devoted to each other and when Hannah died in 1878, Miss Burdett-Coutts told a friend that she was utterly crushed by the loss of 'my poor darling, the companion and sunshine of my life for 52 years'. Talk about a dead giveaway!

Many lesbians then, as now, seem to have been drawn towards the sporting life – though whether by a genuine love of the outdoors or by the lure of the communal showers we will never really know. Harriet Rowell, who in the 1870s taught swimming at Brill's Baths and made quite a local rep for herself by swimming from Shoreham to Brighton in less than three hours through a rough sea (Sapphic metaphors ahoy!), was professionally known as – ahem – Miss Elphinstone Dick. She hooked up with a local gal, Alice Moon, and they emigrated to Australia where they opened a women's gymnasium. Physical jerks drew this pair together, for sure, but who can say whether they were sexual?

But lesbianism in Brighton is not all dog-breeding, antimacassars and joint Christmas cards. It also has its wild side, which thrives on the air of permanent holiday and the temptation to stray from the straight and narrow which living in a seaside town brings with it. My friend K, a lushly gorgeous, smartly soulful 25-year-old girl-about-town, paints a colourful portrait of a town permanently up for it:

> I gave a girl a hand job in a beach hut once. And I had
> this red lipstick on and we were snogging in the loos at

the club (before we left) and when we came out the
cubicle it was all over us – big red kisses all over our
cheeks and cleavage and shoulders. I was wearing this
black strappy dress and you could see it all over my
skin. And I remember thinking, when I looked in the
mirror, how much more beautiful and fun it was to be
a lesbian.

Patrick Hamilton called the West Pier 'that vast sexual
battlefield', and it is this air of Awayday, the-fleet's-in!
recklessness which seems to make bad behaviour even more
irresistible – and somehow natural.

With the sea in sight, it sometimes feels that you are
already in another country – and we all know what the
English abroad are like. You can do things in a resort that
you wouldn't dare do on dry land, so to speak; some writers
have even suggested that once you are on a pier, it's
arguable whether you're in your own land any more
anyway. You're all at sea, with no direction home, and
things that seemed to make sense when you were landlocked
– going to school, getting up for work, staying clean and
sober and straight – seem somehow besides the point now.
As a girl once said to a national radio station phone-in
show I heard, 'I've tried to stop sleeping around – but I live
in Brighton, so it's hard.'

No pun intended, one presumes.

By the 1930s, gay pubs in Brighton were flourishing – the
Star of Brunswick in Brunswick Street West and Pigott's bar
at the St James Tavern in Madeira Place. There were
women-only tea dances at the Royal Albion Hotel and in
1929 the Brighton Man-Woman hit the headlines. Lillias
Arkell-Smith, a lesbian masquerading as Colonel Sir Victor
Ivor Gauntlett Blyth Barker (man-about-town, huntsman
and cricketer), had wooed a Brighton woman, married her

at St Peter's Church and honeymooned at the Grand Hotel. Lillias, regarded by Radclyffe Hall as a 'mad pervert of the most undesirable kind', was found guilty of describing herself as a bachelor in a register of marriage and sentenced to nine months' imprisonment.

Women imitating men went to jail; men imitating women, on the other hand, have always been the belles of the outsiders' ball. But one thing I've never been able to work out in all the times I've stood in various Brighton pubs and clubs lamely applauding some man telling me how much women smell and wondering why I was doing so, is this interesting question: if the Black and White Minstrels, who my good-hearted, non-racist old mum used to love, are allegedly insulting and reactionary, then why aren't drag queens? In all the times I watched them on TV – and twice in the monochrome flesh! – I never saw the BAWMs say that black people are smelly, dumb or sluttish. But I've heard men dressed up as women say it numerous times. A case of 'if you can't join 'em, beat 'em', perhaps, for that minority of misogynist gay men who resent the fact that more men desire women than desire men dressed up as women, and go in for the (if-looks-could) kill accordingly. But everyone, it seems, loves a drag queen in dear old Blighty. Even the vicious and vile men who physically attacked the brilliant and brave Muslim comedienne Shazia Mirza for what they saw as her shamelessness – just after, that is, they had been shrieking with mirth over the antics of a drag queen. And, of course, we indigenous infidels are just as crazy about blokes in frocks, even if we don't usually see fit to beat up defenceless funny girls to make our point.

At the English institution which is the pantomime, a special welcome is always reserved for the Ugly Sisters. Ugly Sisters are, of course, always played by men and, though conventional feminism might look at them askance, I find them oddly appealing and sound; the very fact that no woman, however unattractive, is ever thought to be ugly enough to be an Ugly Sister is a testament to the superior beauty of women. In recent years, we have seen the decline of the Principal Boy, traditionally played by an attractive, athletic girl with extremely good gams; how much of this can be put down to a growing awareness of designer dykery, and our inability to see two pretty girls snogging without putting the worst possible interpretation on it? But you never think of sex when you see the Ugly Sisters.

The best reason for their continuing existence is that they demonstrate how very stupid men look, in fact, when they dress up as women. In the context of panto, this is perfectly appropriate. But for the rest of them, as I've said, I see no difference between transvestite entertainers and the late Black and White Minstrels. They're both extremely offensive, and I don't understand why one is beyond the pale and the other totally acceptable in enlightened circles.

And, yes, I know that they're not the same, but may I say that I feel even less patience with transsexuals. Male-to-female transsexuals are Michael Jackson to the transvestites Ali G; not content even to dress up temporarily as the Other, they presume that its authenticity can be theirs through a few cosmetic adjustments. We laugh at people who want to change colour; we are shocked that millions of Japanese women each year have their eyes permanently occidentalised; we ban skin-lightening preparations, and would never dream of letting black people have Jackson-type whitening operations on the NHS. Yet we pay for thousands of men every year to 'become' women: around 7,000 at £8,000 a pop, and rising every year. You do the maths. 'Oh, but I'm a woman trapped in a man's body!' So? What about all the white people who feel black, black people who feel white, poor people with rich people's tastes and short people who are dying to be tall? They're all welcome to go off and seek to make their dreams a reality, but I don't see the NHS spending money that could be better spent on hip operations, cancer treatments and simply cleaning up our filthy hospitals. The NHS was never designed to be a sort of state-run *Jim'll Fix It*, and I don't understand why gender must be the one exception.

The *Daily Mail* seems to have a special, not quite wholesome interest in male-to-female transsexuals, featuring at least one a month in extensive Before and After poses, with a headline typically saying something like THE PUBLIC SCHOOL SIR WHO WANTS TO BE A MISS; Nicholas/Nicola the Charterhouse teacher, Ian/Isabelle the Oxford tutor, Bill/Dian the Welsh preacher and Simon/Carol the C of E vicar. Its attitude used to be that these people were dangerous sexual radicals; now, it seeks to portray them as tragic victims.

My objection to trannies, though, is that they are woefully conventional souls (typical *Mail* readers, in fact) who seem unable to exist alongside any sort of ambiguity, which as we all know is one of the things that makes life so interesting. I wouldn't have the least problem leaving a young girl child in the care of any of them – I'd fear sexual molestation far less than from a 'straight' man – but I would be worried that, by the time I came home, the child would be dressed from head to toe in pink and being danced round the room to the saccharine strains of 'Thank Heaven for Little Girls'.

It is the literal-mindedness, the clunky logic of transsexuals, that is so appalling (that, and their taste in blouses), not their sexual depravity. They are frilly, docile smilers who always wear makeup and never the trousers. Their idea of womanhood seems to have survived intact from 1953. Despite their sticky lipstick rictuses, they are the ultimate example of a particularly middle-class, middle-aged male arrogance that cannot see why anything it desires shouldn't be so. Such men invariably report that they were aware of feeling 'trapped' in the wrong body since boyhood. Yet, thoughtfully, they go ahead and marry blissfully ignorant women and father children. Then, in middle age, with the kids off their hands, and when their wives are looking forward to kicking back and relaxing *à deux*, she comes home one day from Marks & Spencer to find hubby prancing about in her second-best Frank Usher frock and committing GBH on her new Carvela kitten heels. These poor stunned women – talk about feeling you've been sold a pup! – are then told by the caring professionals and counsellors to accept their husbands as 'sisters'.

Just switch it for a moment and imagine that thousands of women decided they wanted penises. Would their husbands be expected to stay with them and live as brothers? Somehow, I doubt it. But it seems that whatever men choose to do – be it buy pornography from sweetshops, masturbate at impoverished single mothers on 'chatlines', walk naked in the street (as Vincent Bethell was given the right to do recently) or demand to be called Daphne – must at all costs be normalised, whereas, for women, the rules are all but unshifting.

Transsexualism is, basically, just another, more drastic twist on the male menopause, which in turn is just another excuse for men to do as they please. And before the geek chorus – hi fans! – start up, yes, I know I've been pretty damned selfish during my long and squalid marital career. The difference is, of course, that I've never sought to dress up my own egoism in poor-me-trapped-in-the-wrong-life claptrap, and I've certainly never expected the taxpayer to hand over more than £8,000 in order to set me up in a love nest with my new squeeze. No – at the end of the day, changing sex is no more noble than changing your wife for a new woman. Only, this time, the woman is you.

The strand of misogyny which runs through gay male culture is slender but constant, from the old Arab gag 'A woman for duty, a boy for pleasure and a melon for ecstasy', through the phenomenon of fag hags – adored and mocked in the same breath – to the ever-charming Stephen Fry and his highly appropriate quote about his mother's vagina and his own homosexuality – 'I suppose it all began when I came out of the womb. I looked back up at my mother and thought to myself: that's the last time I'm going up one of those.'

The list of gay male hate/thought crimes against women is shameful and shady; even a minority of those active in the fight against AIDS seemed to have learned little or no compassion towards their sisters. In the 1980s, when the Western establishment was doing its level best to de-segregate AIDS and make it an issue of general sexual behaviour rather than just a gay one – as indeed gay spokesmen had insisted was vital to its treatment – there were, astoundingly, gay men who grew quite spiteful and selfish on being asked to 'share', as it were. The American gay activist Leo Bersani described early Public Information Broadcasts as 'a nauseating procession of Yuppie women announcing to the world that they will no longer put out to their Yuppie boyfriends unless they use a condom. Thus hundreds of thousands of gay men and IV drug users are asked to sympathize with all these Yuppettes agonizing over whether they're going to risk a good fuck by taking the "unfeminine" initiative of interrupting the invading male in order to insist that he practice safe sex.'

It was this sort of filthy gaynaephobia that made the great American feminist Marilyn Frye write in 1983, 'Gay men generally are in significant ways, perhaps in all important ways, more loyal to masculinity and male-supremacy than other men. The gay rights movement may be the fundamentalism of the global religion which is patriarchy.' While not in the same league as the rape, assault and domestic violence and murder the little ladies are privy to from a minority of straight men, the behaviour of certain gay men dots the i's and crosses the t's of misogyny. We see this in Brighton especially, as gay men are emboldened by their multiplicity; in some nightclubs where gay men are the majority and straight women the minority (gay women and straight men have the good sense to stay away), some boys will at the end of an evening, if they haven't had the good fortune to cop off with a fellow fellow, enquire boldly of individual phallically challenged camp followers present, 'Do you want to give me a handjob, or what?'

How the flighty have fallen! And what a sad decline of standards from when, back in the day, the gay lexicon 'Polari' ruled the roost as the most imaginative, vivid slang ever to grace these isles. Its name came from the typically luscious Italian word 'to talk', and from the nineteenth century to the 1960s it was a truly diverse – that is, organically diverse, without any fingers wagging or liberals nagging – voice. Made up of Italian, Romany, Cockney, Yiddish, criminal, druggie, GI and sailor slang, it invented more than five hundred words and, from 'alamo' (sexually attracted to) to 'zhooshy' (flashy) each one was a gem, polished and sharpened by the homo-hostility of the times. With typical clod-hopping humourlessness, the gay 'liber-ationists' of the 1970s saw Polari as shameful and politically incorrect – as opposed to slyly triumphant, which it was – and this gorgeous lingo was banished by the self-appointed leaders of the 'gay community'. In its place came the somewhat sordid Handkerchief Code – red for fisting, yellow for watersports, blue for blowjobs and green for payment. And, no doubt, beige to indicate someone really, really boring, taupe for someone with a yen for interior decorators and mauve to warn potential suitors that this is a maudlin mister who enjoys nothing more than a good old cry at Bette Davis films. When I think of luscious Polari being ousted by crude hanky-flashing, I think of what the great John Cooper Clark once whispered in my ear as we watched a roomful of old hippies letting it all hang out: 'Repression is the mother of the metaphor.'

Of course, everyone's got a right to be out and proud. But I can't think that it makes more sense to be proud of one's actual achievements rather than to be proud merely of what one is born as; after all, that was just a random occurrence, and if everyone from blacks to gays to women can say they are 'proud' to be so, doesn't it apply equally that people can, equally pathetically, be proud to be white, heterosexual or men? Which, from where I'm sitting, leaves just a huge mess of people running round being needlessly, defensively, separately 'proud'; 'divisive' and 'hysterical' are two more words that spring to mind here, I'm afraid.

I mean, I love living in Brighton – but I'd never be so silly as to say I was proud of being a Brightonian. Who could be proud of a place where public conveniences have all but been turned into cafés and flower shops due to the fact that their colonisation by gay men searching for a quick hand-shandy made them unviable? Like Polari and hankies, it seems a shame that liberation brought with it a decline in standards – and that's not homophobic, because I would also say that any woman or straight man who hung around toilets looking for sex was also a total skank. Personally, I'm like a camel when it comes to water-holding capacity, but it does seem unfair to me that old people and the incontinent generally should have to suffer the consequences of toilets becoming trysting places. I mean, we've all heard of the Pink Pound – we know they've got homes to go to. There's just something very uber-male, as Marilyn Frye implied, about this tomcattish desire to mark territory, albeit with sperm rather than urine. (And they said romance was dead!)

And it's not just the lavvies, which, let's face it, weren't that salubrious to begin with. But was it really necessary to turn Hove Lawns into an alfresco shag-palace? No wonder the poor Peace Angel turned to stone, all the things she must have seen! At least with the advent of 'The Bushes'@ 'Duke's Mound' – a bit of scrubland on the seafront going towards the Marina, which of course every non-Brightonian thinks you made up the name of – there came a place which no woman or child could ever have taken pleasure in anyway. (Unless they were those ones who're raised by wolves, without a TV and stuff, and like they never get over it.) It did seem of bit off that there used to be a council-paid cleaner who was employed exclusively to get rid of the detritus of the previous night's sexcesses – let's hope it was a gay man having to clear up after all those fellow gay men because having a hetero, male or female, would somehow seem to be taking the piss in more ways than one. But since it seems to now operate 24/7, it's an alleged clean-up-as-you-come environment. There is even a thoughtfully pro-vided 'Condom Van' from the local Outreach Project, which visits at the rush hour in the late evening.

But still the few toilets that are open prove a lure too great to resist. 'There is no such thing as society', eh boyz! When Mrs Thatcher said that she was being a right cow, to listen to the same right-ons who condone khazi-cruising, but when gayers choose to inconvenience the public in public conveniences, suddenly it's all fine and dandy. What a relief to realise that it's not only heteros who are hypocrites when it comes to sex!

When heteros are hypocritical about sex, the sort of sex they tend to be very hypocritical about is prostitution. I must say here that I don't approve of prostitution as I don't believe that the good Lord made us in his image so that we could act as sexual spittoons hired out by the half-hour for all and sundry to use. But in a hate-the-sin, love-the-sinner sort of way, which is unusual for me, I would also say it is a fact that sex workers can be lovely women – and it's hardly them who are the sinners, in my view, but rather the seat-sniffers who frequent them.

A little story, here, about a sex worker. ('Whore' makes it sound like they enjoy it and don't wash, 'hooker' makes them sound like they hang out in fishnets along the Strip trading wisecracks with hard-bitten but basically good-hearted cops, 'call-girl' makes them sound like they sit on cream-coloured sofas flicking through Vogue and waiting for cream-coloured phones to ring, while 'working girl' is just plain vain – we most of us work, ladies!) Anyway, when I made my handsome profit by flogging my detached pile in Hove to a moustache-twirling developer at the start of 2006, this just happened to coincide with a dramatic escalation in My Christian Journey – and ever since then, predictably but oh-so-pleasurably, I've gone around flinging money at favoured causes, charities and individuals like a sailor on shore-leave. Amongst my friends, I've proffered sums between £4,000 and £30,000 and with only one exception they have, quite naturally, accepted. All except one; my sex worker friend of more than a decade, who now finds herself fiftysomething, in rented accommodation, with a rather large tax-shaped Sword of Damocles hovering over her immaculate head. And did she take the modest £10,000 I offered her? No; instead she said 'Scamp! How many times must I tell you not to fling your money around! Save it for a rainy day!' It's not meant to tug on your heartstrings; it's just a story. Albeit a true one.

Anyway, that's my attitude towards prostitution; now back to the hypocrites. Now, in my experience it's common wisdom that there is only one way to be a filthy hypocrite about prostitution, and that is to thunder against it in public while slipping around to get a slice in private. Naturally, when these jokers are banged to rights, we all enjoy it, because to criticise someone/something and then do them/it is just plain creepy. And it makes you look like seven kinds of saddo thinking that you'll be the very first one not to get caught! Who do you think you are, dude? Mr Invisible Man? This is the trad kind of prost-hyp – Disgusted of Tunbridge Wells, if you will – humphing about moral decline over his *Daily Telegraph* on the commuter train, then nipping out at lunchtime to have Vera from Vladivostock void her vowels over him. But there's another type of prost-hyp around these days – we'll call him Horrified of Hampstead. He's a liberal sort of chap who says that prostitution is fine, so long as his mother, daughters, wives, sisters and – *especially* perish the thought! – sons aren't doing it. And, on balance, I think I find this second type of hypocrisy more offensive and ridiculous, as H.O.H. invariably considers himself so incredibly enlightened.

Yes, just as the *Telegraph* will feature some sweet old buffer who has seen the first crocus of the year, so the *Guardian* letters page will annually feature the first MEP of the year who has just seen his first legalised European brothel and has to share it with the rest of us. Unreconstructed feminist I may be, but whenever I hear any man suggest that prostitution can be anything other than a degrading, soul-destroying blight and should be made more socially acceptable, I have to smile nicely and say, 'And would you like your wife to work as a paid whore, sir? Or your daughter? *Or indeed your son, sir?* On his back, feet up in stirrups – your little birthday boy with the candles gleaming in his shiny-make-a-wish eyes! – with the pox-doctor's clammy glove up his arse having a right old root around? Hang on, but you approved of regular state health checks for sex workers just a minute ago!'

The gender agenda is a weird one; men really want to believe in the myth of the 'happy hooker': 'Lots of them have orgasms with their clients, sometimes multiple!' – that'd be with *you*, would it, dude, that day you bought them a pair of shoes on top of the flat fee? But rent boys are invariably 'damaged'. Logically, this differing attitude to sex work doesn't make the slightest sense as men are generally so much more promiscuous and interested in anonymous sex than women, gay men even more so. One can only imagine that when a straight man thinks about rent boys, he experiences one of those there-but-for-the grace, goose-walked-over-my-grave moments as he imagines himself renting his body to a leering parade of unattractive strangers to use as they will for a pittance. A bit like, um, female sex workers do, in fact – there's a thing!

Yep, somehow, prostitution-enthusers don't see it quite the same way when they think about their mum or their son doing it. It's an instinctive, and I believe appropriate response. Other jobs may be unpleasant, but none of us would really be ashamed to say that one of our loved ones was a drains inspector, undertaker or toilet attendant. I venture that most of us would, however, shrink from revealing at parties that our children or relatives were prostitutes, no matter how clean and legal their brothel. This is because we instinctively realise that prostitution is vile and exploitative. But it will always exist, so long as vice is rewarded so much better than virtue. The fact that some nurses work as part-time prostitutes in order to finance their own goodness-in-action, for instance, I find peculiarly and repulsively mind-blowing. That most elegant and discreet of Brighton sex workers, Letitcia, was asked by Brighton and Hove council to take part in an initiative for the proposed creation of 'mini brothels': 'I filled in this extensive questionnaire and was paid £5 for my trouble. Since it took me an hour to complete, I feel I am still owed £145!'

The Swedes, who tend to know a bit about sex, have the right idea; it is a crime to pay for sex anywhere, from anyone, but *not* to sell it. Christian soldier that I am, I'm also a realist and know very well that my sex worker friends would scream blue murder if this happened, but equally, they are totally opposed to state-run brothels. This isn't just about wanting to avoid tax, either; it's about the fact that in countries where prostitution is state-regulated, women who become sex workers find it very difficult to become anything else. Under these 'liberal' set-ups, paradoxically, you're marked for life. In Germany, partly because of this, it is thought that only 12 per cent of sex workers frequent the creepily named state-regulated 'Eros Zones', and prefer to live illegally rather than let the state act as their pimp. Disgustingly, in Germany, if a woman with a past as a prostitute is receiving benefits the state can actually force her to take a job in a brothel; if she refuses, her benefits automatically stop. Mind you, attempting to herd, control and exploit women who have fallen on hard times is hardly new in Germany; Hitler himself presided over state-regulated brothels as a key institution of the bogus Nazi 'cleanliness' kick. (A healthy mind in a healthy body, my arse; hmm, that'll be why his soldiers wore hats with skulls on them!)

Britons, on the other hand, never never never shall be slaves, and it is one of the relatively good things about prostitution in this country, unregulated as it is, that sex workers need not be stuck in the cage forever. Especially in Brighton, with its free-wheeling transience and its expense-account conferences, I have known people who act as seasonal prostitutes – a weekend here, a night there – and then go back to their lives as everything from shop assistants to mature students. Thus sex work is what they occasionally do, but sex workers is not what they define themselves as. It's not ideal, but it's a good sight better than being branded for life, and thus forced to remain on the horizontal treadmill forever. I should say here that, sadly, this only applies to indigenous sex workers; trafficked women from overseas have no such luck. But even this is an evil which is perpetuated by over-liberal immigration policies rather than by prostitution itself; the 23 Chinese cockle-pickers who died to profit gangmasters in Morecombe Bay were victims of the same open-door idiocy as the frightened teenagers from Albania being raped by two dozen punters a day.

So all in all it would be a rotten day indeed for this country if the state ever became the biggest pimp of all, and no woman was ever allowed to make a fresh start after a spell in the skin trade. Of course, lap-dancing and prostitution are a world apart, but they do count as opposite ends of the sex industry. To be coarse about it, hands-off sex work for the young and pretty, and hands-on sex work for the rest. Whatever, it was lovely to read a letter to the *Argus* in November 2006 from an alarmingly pretty girl – 'Courtney' – whose barely clad photograph had appeared the day before. Under the heading LIFE HAS CHANGED, the mystery girl wrote the following:

An article published yesterday in *The Argus* on the general topic of lap-dancing clubs also featured a photograph of me taken during a brief stint as a lap-dancer at the Pussycat Club in Hove under the stage name I used at the time, Courtney.

I would like to point out the picture was taken five years ago. I only took on that line of work for a few months and have not done so since. I'm pleased to say I now live a very happy family life and enjoy a very different role as the mother of a four-year-old girl and that I'm pregnant with another child on the way. My life and work could not be more different since that time as, along with my role as a parent, I now work in an office.

I hope that makes matters clear.

Name and address supplied

Call me a sentimental old fool, but I definitely welled up a bit when I read that. At a time when so many middle-class women who have never felt the economic pressure to make 'easy' money talk about pole- or lap-dancing as if *all* it was was a jolly good wheeze/extremely empowering, this beautiful young woman's sense of pride and propriety was a breath of fresh air.   Without once getting the out violins or the victimisation status, she named what she had done and took herself back without shame, apology or compromise – pointing out that making a living from one's youth and beauty is not *always*, is not *only* a cause for triumphalism. Though, as with the example of Jordan, it certainly can be. But for girls whose nature is unsuited to public display, being up there on the podium can be about being at the bottom, treading water in the shallow end of the sex trade for a while, not grinding but drowning. And if a modern young woman can feel this way, imagine what turmoil was taking place in the heads of the pin-up/postcard pornography models of the past, their desperation made picturesque by the benediction of sepia.

Distance lends cosiness to many rotten things. Visitors to London are offered numerous 'Jack the Ripper Tours', from Gray Line London Tours alone a basic walk for £21 – 'An actor takes you around the very same streets, recapturing the horror and mystery of those dark nights' – and a slash'n'mash deluxe job for £28 – 'Turn this tour into a spectacular night out with our dinner option. After the tour we will call at the Albert, a typical 19th century English pub, where you can sample fish-and-chips, or a main course of your choice, followed by dessert.' A banquet eaten off of the mutilated bodies of dead prostitutes isn't really my thing, but whatever turns you on. Similarly, when we look at the (then) living bodies of the plump young prostitutes of the past, with their corsets and their coquettish turn-of-the-century eyes, we don't see the undertones of exploitation, fear and loneliness that it is easy enough for us to perceive in some modern pornography; the past is a foreign country, where hurting can pass as flirting. When we consider that even unmarried mothers were treated as filthy, fallen women into the middle of the twentieth century, what a big and frightening decision it must have been for a young girl to become a pin-up/prostitute – because back then, with those hardcore hateful sex-morals, one surely led to the other. There was none of the freedom to move back and forth between lap-dancing and decency that the bold young Courtneys of today enjoy.

The past seems so cosy, if we just allow ourselves to turn off our minds and float into the seductive slipstream of historical Hovis-ad ignorance for just a few minutes. Sex during the Edwardian and Victorian eras is often reinter-preted as a whole barrel-organ of maid-chasing, ass-slap-ping, no-harm-done fun, in some sort of alternative 'pure' state before the stifling paws of PC got its hands on it. But for every smirking sex journal of some mutton-chopped 'gentleman', gloating over his ability to use a Whitechapel waif as a spunk-bucket for a handful of pennies on his way home to the smug suburbs – there, perchance, to give syphilis to his unsuspecting wife – there were a thousand scared, cold, lonely girls and women whose next customer had every likelihood of being Jack the Ripper. Like I said before, don't say such a life is fine for anyone, unless you include your mother, your son, your sister, yourself.

Yet when we see the Edwardian and Victorian pin-ups, we see their plumpness and their smiles, and because of it we cannot seen their hunger and sadness, knowing that they will never go home – back to their old home, or onward to create a new home – again, for they are outcasts living with the stinking, hypocritical morality of those times. That such women should be sometimes known as 'good-time girls' is a misnomer beyond belief.

Brighton, being a saucy seaside resort, can gloss over the history of its prostituted women as slickly as anywhere. From the dawn of the railway age punters seeking both men and women flocked from London, since the going rate here is substantially lower than in the capital – the old saw 'London prices, Brighton wages' for once not being entirely the case, unfortunately for the benighted sex workers. By 1859 there were almost four hundred brothels in Brighton – and can't the very word 'brothel', at this distance, lull one into conjuring up a welcoming haven glimpsed through a pea-souper night (*come on in out of the cold and slip into a warm piece of pussy!*) – rather than the misery factories they more than likely were.

In Brighton, the inevitable Carry On air hung over what was essentially a wretched business, which no sentient woman given a chance to make the same sort of money standing would choose. During the blackout Brighton tarts wore red hats, giving rise to the expression, 'Red hat – no knickers.' As the post-war world settled down and suited up, the town was regularly awash with businessmen away from home, and with the 1977 opening of the 4,500-seater Brighton Centre, the expense account shag came into its own. Or rather, someone else's. And the rise of the quaintly named 'Escort Agency' fitted in well with this Play-Away-Day ethos.

I've been bigging-up sex workers against my better judgement no end here, so I'll take this oppo to showcase my comfortingly bitchy side. And I'll paraphrase Winston Churchill on the Russians: 'They can be trusted when they wear their shirts outside of their trousers, but not when they tuck them in.' I think he was saying that the essential nature of the Russian was Eastern rather than Western; I have no idea whether this is true or not, but I would tweak the advice a little in this context to say of sex workers, 'They can be trusted when they call themselves prostitutes –

but when they call themselves escorts, keep an eye on your handbag!' Basically, if someone can't be honest about what they do to make a living . . . And the one thing these people certainly don't do is 'escort' people anywhere, apart from the bedroom, as the last thing the people paying them want is to be seen with them. Harsh but true!

Still, sweetness has a way of raising its dazed head in the most sleazy of environments. One of these early 'escort agencies' was situated in George Street (Kemp Town) and run by an apparently relatively sweet man. Punters flocked up the spiral staircase to pay an 'agency fee' of £25; this was necessary since the 'fee' absolved the agency of any nefarious goings on when the protagonists met. There was just one problem. The owner kept falling in love with his girls and therefore would take them off the books in the time-honoured 'No woman of *mine* is going to sleep with a paying customer!' tradition. What a sweet reminder of a time before the modern habit of calling oneself a 'pimp' and one's paramour a 'ho' became the height of romantic display!

Prostitution is nothing if not market-led, and the privatisation of British Telecom gave sex workers a new outlet in which to advertise their services – 'Carding'; a mode of announcing 'availability' which was peculiar only to Brighton, the city of Westminster and Glasgow. (Though there have been outcrops on the coast of Lincolnshire, due no doubt to the transient maritime population.)

'Carding' was a haphazard occupation; as soon as they were placed in phone boxes, either a cleaner or a policeman might pop up citing 'destruction and littering'. Prostitutes often worked in pairs, with one as 'lookout'; turf wars developed and rival workers would have their cards 'pulled'. The cards became ever cruder as the doxies became desperate to stand out from the crowd; my own sex worker chum had the grace to look rather sheepish when she told me, 'I stupidly tried cards as a form of advertising for about five weeks and made the mistake of attempting humour. Sadly, my IF YOU PAY PEANUTS YOU GET MONKEYS! cards – complete with a cartoon of two orangutans – did not find the other working ladies in Brighton best pleased.'

Brighton Museum now has a display of these cards for the purposes of cultural and historical interest. And, 'oldest profession' or not, what a wonderful dawn it would be when every shameful shackle of the sex trade – like the slave trade before it, which with the rise of open-door immigration and the trading of women fresh off the planes on the actual tarmac of British airports it is coming more and more to resemble – can be found only in the glass cases of museums.

But until then, mine's a top table at the front of the first all-nude Brighton lap-dancing club, champagne on ice and a wad of fifties at the ready, sad slave to beauty that I am.

THE HISTORY OF BRIGHTON:
AN AT-TIMES-ARBITRARY TIMELINE

(The authors wish to gratefully acknowledge Eric Underwood's excellent book *Brighton* (Batsford, 1978), from which many of the bare facts and most of the quotes in this section have been shamelessly pilfered.)

3000 BC Approximate date for the construction of Whitehawk Hill causewayed camp – the oldest known settlement in the Brighton area. The camp most likely served as a kind of al fresco community centre, a venue for meetings, markets and religious observance. Bit of a touchy-feely, New Agey sort of place, then? Er, no: when the site was excavated by E. Cecil Curwen in 1928 he discovered the charred remains of at least five people – one of them no bigger than a six-year-old – who had very obviously been *cooked* and *eaten*!

1500 BC A new wave of immigrants from the Continent arrives in the area, bringing with them fancy new ways of farming and metalworking (the 'Brighton loop' bracelet design begins to appear at around this time).

500 BC More immigrants arrive from north-western Europe with the new metal 'iron', which quickly supersedes bronze. The first hill forts appear (most famously at Hollingbury).

AD 43 Rome invades south-eastern England, but the belt of land between Lewes and Chichester (including what is now Brighton) is mysteriously spared any hostilities. The most likely cause is that a local big shot pledged his support to Rome in advance of the invasion. He is ultimately rewarded for his efforts with a huge palace at Fishbourne in AD 75–80.

275 After roughly two centuries of presumed *pax romana* (all we know of the Romans' involvement with the area is that there were large houses or farms in Preston, Southwick and West Blatchington), barbarian tribes begin to intermittently attack the South Coast.

410 The Britons ask the Roman Emperor Honorius for help against a Saxon invasion – the last occupying Roman soldier having left Britain three years before – and are told they will have to 'look after their own defences'. This they do, holding off the invaders so successfully that by AD 430 they are employing Saxons as mercenaries in battles against the Picts and the Scots.

442 The Saxons rebel against their British employers (oh the ingratitude!). In 457 they welcome reinforcements from home under the leadership of a fella named Aella, who proceeds to conquer the whole region; this subsequently becomes known as the land of the South Saxons, or Sussex. Some historians contend that Aella was only prevented from conquering further territories by the intervention of King Arthur!

675(ish) Sussex becomes the last of the Anglo-Saxon kingdoms to be converted to Christianity, by St Wilfred. The name Brighthelmstone may derive from the name of one of Wilfred's priests – 'Beorthelm's-tun', meaning 'Beorthelm's farm'.

1066 William the Conqueror invades Britain; contemporary accounts indicate that Brighton's peasantry accepts the change of management with little more than a token show of peevishness. The Domesday Book of 1086 records that

Brighton (or 'Bristelmstune') is divided into three manors, each owned by one of William de Warrene (Will the Conk's son-in-law)'s knights. The town itself is little more than a small warren of alleyways – roughly covering the area now known as the Lanes – with St Nicholas' Church set back from the other buildings on a steep hill, ready to serve as a fortress in the event of invasion.

1341 For tax purposes, Brighton tells emissaries of Edward III that 'forty acres [of land have been] submerged forever' by the sea over the last fifty years.

1513 French forces under the leadership of Admiral Pregent (known as 'Prior John' in common parlance) land at 'a poore village called Bright Helmston', plundering and torching it before apparently being driven back to their boats by angry locals with bows and arrows.

1545 A contemporary map of Brighton shows one hundred houses in the area now bordered by North Street, East Street and West Street, arranged around a central field where hemp is grown for the fishermen's nets. Hove comprises just twelve houses and a church.

On 18 July another French Admiral, Claude d'Annebaut, 'with his whole Navy (which consisted of two hundred ships and twenty-six gallies) came forth into the seas, and arrived on the coast of Sussex before Bright Hamstead, and set certain of his soldiers on land to burn and spoil the country: but the beacons were fired, and the inhabitants thereabouts came down so thick, that the Frenchmen were driven to flie with loss of diverse of their numbers: so that they did little hurt there'.

1642 During the Civil War the people of Sussex predominantly side with Parliament against the Crown, although leaders on both sides are moved to comment on the half-hearted attitude of their Sussex troops.

1651 The George Inn (which no longer exists, but probably stood in either Middle or West Street) plays host to King Charles II, travelling incognito in the final stages of a plan to smuggle him out of the country. The innkeeper recognises him but swears not to tell anyone, adding that he hopes to receive a lordship in return some day. The next morning Charles escapes on the coal-brig *Surprise*, which had been beached somewhere between Brighton and Shoreham.

1676 Erosion of the town's chalk cliffs and shingle beaches continues to be a problem as more and more buildings are swept away. William Jeffrey, a Brighton yeoman, tells the Justices of the Peace at Lewes that 'in case there be not a peere or some other speedy course taken for the security of the sd port all or the most parte of the said Towne and p'ish of Brighthelmston will be in danger of being swallowed up by the raging of the sea. The charge of wch peer or other security to the port will amount to the sume of 7000£ att the least.' This 'sume' amounts to nearly £2 million in today's money; the pier is not immediately forthcoming . . .

1722 George I issues a 'Church Brief' or 'King's Letter' authorising churches throughout England to take a collection for the construction of groynes (stone breakwaters) at Brighton.

1724 Daniel Defoe's *A Tour Through the Whole Island of Great Britain* describes the Sussex county town of Lewes as 'a fine pleasant town, well built, agreeably situated'. By contrast, 'Bright Helmston, commonly called Bredhemston' is 'a poor fishing town, old built, and on the very edge of the sea. The sea is very unkind to this town, and has by its continual encroachments, so gained upon them, that in a little more they might reasonably expect it would eat up the whole town, above 100 houses having been devoured by the water in a few years past; they are now obliged to get a brief granted them, to beg money all over England, to raise banks against the water; the expense of which, the brief expressly says, will be eight thousand pounds which if one were to look on the town, would seem to be more than all the houses in it are worth.'

1744 Bright Helmston now comprises 454 households, three-quarters of which are exempt from paying rates due to extreme poverty.

1750 Oxford University Press publishes Dr Richard Russell's *De Tabe Glandulari: Sive Usu Aquae Marinae in Morbis Glandularum* – 'Glandular Diseases, or a Dissertation on the Use of Sea Water in Affections of the Glands'. The book is an instant smash both with medical professionals and, when the author's own translation appears three years later (following the appearance of an unauthorised 'bootleg' version), the general reading public. It recommends drinking and bathing in sea-water as a curative for a whole range of maladies, but the main focus is on consumption (TB). Russell's medical practice happens to be in Lewes, so patients prescribed the sea cure are inevitably sent to Brighton. News of the town's healing waters soon spreads as sea-bathing becomes a craze among the rich and fashionable . . .

1759 Dr Russell dies.

1771 The Duke of Cumberland (brother to King George III) becomes Brighton's latest high-born habitué, renting an imposing house on the seafront previously occupied by the unfortunate Dr Russell (now the site of the Royal Albion Hotel). His recent marriage to an Irish widow has elicited criticism from the King himself, but he finds solace in the company of what the *Morning Herald* calls a 'motley group', which enthusiastically pursues 'every kind of amusement that fancy can desire for the train of folly and dissipation'.

1779 The town now comprises 600–700 houses. Peregrine Phillips, author of *Bew's Diary*, writes of visiting a friend's home in Brighton at this time: 'The ground on which it stands is . . . nearly eighteen feet square . . . About fifty years ago this piece of land was sold for four pounds; thirty years since, a purchaser gave eleven; and about this time two years, the Alderman bought it for one hundred pounds.'

1783 On 7 September, George, Prince of Wales (the heir to the throne), who has fallen in with the Duke of Cumberland as a result of their shared enmity towards the King, visits Brighton for the first time. The occasion is marked by the ringing of bells at St Nicholas' Church and a round of cannon-fire from the battery on the seafront; a gunner is killed when one of the cannon charges goes off too soon.

1785 Prince George marries twice-widowed Mrs Maria Fitzherbert in London. The ceremony is held in secret; George cannot marry without his father's consent until he is 25, and there is no chance of the King allowing his son and heir to marry a Catholic. Subsequently the couple divide their time between London and Brighton, keeping separate residences in each town (though they are regarded as a legitimate couple everywhere but at Court). In Brighton, Mrs Fitzherbert takes a house on the Steine (now the YMCA . . .!) while George has a large Italianate villa ('the Pavilion') a few dozen yards inland.

1793 The outbreak of yet another war with France. Brighton is ringed with tented barracks and becomes a hidey-hole of choice for fleeing French aristos.

1794 Prince George abandons Mrs Fitzherbert in order to marry Caroline of Brunswick, a German princess. His motivation is purely financial: he has debts of around £375,000 which his father will not pay unless a Protestant bloodline is secured.

1795 Two soldiers are shot dead by a firing squad and two more brutally flogged at Goldstone Valley following an insurgence sparked by poor quality rations.

The night before his marriage to Caroline, Prince George asks his brother to 'tell Mrs Fitzherbert she is the only woman I shall ever love'.

1800 Over the last thirty years the number of houses in Brighton has doubled – from around 650 to nearly 1,300. About a third of these offer some form of rented accommodation for visitors to the town. Not all the new properties are Regency masterpieces – in *Brighton: Old Ocean's Bauble* (Flare Books, 1975), Professor Edmund W. Gilbert notes: 'the slum areas of Brighton were in all respects as bad as those of the industrial towns of the north'.

After five years of advancing melancholy and ill health, Prince George heeds the entreaties of – among others – the Queen herself by reuniting with Mrs Fitzherbert. Though they presumably have little choice but to at least tolerate each other, Mrs F. and Caroline of Brunswick surprise everyone by becoming firm friends.

1806 A civil engineer called Ralph Dodd wins the distinction of being the first of very, very many to propose a Marina at Brighton. The plan gains the support of the fishermen but the opposition of the town's 'valetudinarians' (rich ill people); it is soon quietly laid to rest.

1808 J. B. Otto, a West Indian entrepreneur, builds Royal Crescent and so becomes the first to develop Brighton east of the Steine. By 1818, nearly half of all Brighton's houses will be east of the Steine.

1811 Prince George becomes Regent and almost immediately dumps Mrs Fitzherbert yet again, replacing her with the conspicuously Protestant Marchioness of Hertford. Contemporary rumours suggest that either or both of Mrs F.'s 'adopted daughters' were, in fact, George's issue; the couple may also have smuggled a son off to America.

1815 Following the successful completion of the Moorish-looking Royal Stables and Riding House (now the Dome/Corn Exchange) in 1808, the Prince Regent abandons an earlier (1803) plan to redesign the Pavilion in the style of a Chinese pagoda and commissions John Nash (designer of London's Regent Street) to deliver the ultimate Indian takeaway instead. The remodelling is completed in 1821, to the near-universal derision of Brightonians.

1821 Railings are put up around the Steine, and Brighton's fishermen are told to find somewhere else to dry their nets.

1822 King's Road, Brighton's first seafront carriageway, is opened to traffic.

1823 The Chain Pier is completed. Designed by Captain Samuel Brown, the pier – 'a model of grace combined with solidity', according to one foreign visitor – proves not solid enough for Brighton's tides and is repeatedly damaged by storms, eventually succumbing altogether in 1896.

Thomas Read Kemp, a lord of the manor of Brighton and former MP for Lewes, starts work on the construction of Kemp Town. He has noticed that Brighton lacks an estate of houses big enough to attract the truly wealthy and envisages something on the scale of what Nash is building in London.

1827 The fishermen riot, angered by the continued erosion of their historic rights. Ninety-three shopkeepers from North Street, sworn in as special constables on the spot, manage to suppress them.

George IV (the King formerly known as Prince George) abandons his Pavilion and Brighton itself, never to return; the cause of his flight remains a mystery. The Duke of Wellington later asserts that the departure was instigated by George's new mistress – one Lady Conyngham – after she read some unfavourable graffiti about herself on a window. Unhelpfully, the Duke fails to report what the inflammatory message actually was.

1831 The town's population now stands at 40,600.

1837 Financial difficulties force Thomas Read Kemp to flee the country with Kemp Town only half finished. He settles in Paris and dies seven years later. Queen Victoria ascends to the throne and becomes an occasional visitor to Brighton.

1841 Work on the London to Brighton railway line is completed three years after it commenced. The first journey of a train along the new route occasions wild excitement, according to the *Brighton Herald*: 'Parties of ladies and gentlemen were formed on every brow, and every field and meadow, from Preston to Withdean and Patcham, had its mass of human life. It was along these elevated points, which look down on the railroad, that the approach of the train was first perceived, and at about twenty minutes after twelve it was announced to those from whose sight it was yet hid by the winding of the hills by a thousand cries of "Here they come!" '

One month later a train leaves the tracks twelve miles to the north of Brighton, killing two – but this has little to no impact on the railway's popularity. The London to Brighton coach trade will be rendered practically non-existent within three years.

1845 On 8 February, Queen Victoria and Prince Albert take a stroll to the Chain Pier, devoid of retinue. The *Sunday Times* of 9 February reports: 'From (the pier) to the Palace is somewhat more than 100 yards, and while this space was being traversed by royalty some curious and impertinent visitors (we have never recognised among the parties who have thus acted any of the *inhabitants* of Brighton) pressed round her Majesty and her royal consort, some of them even pressing beneath the royal bonnet ... This annoyance to the Queen is a disgrace to the town. The persons who surrounded the Queen were chiefly tradesmen's boys ... with baskets on their arms.' (Presumably tradesmen's boys didn't really count as *inhabitants* of Brighton ...) The Queen leaves town later that month and steers well clear for the next twenty years.

1848 In his *Popular Lectures on the Prevailing Diseases of Towns*, Dr William Kebbel describes the new slum areas around Edward Street as 'a disgrace to any civilised people'.

Queen Victoria removes all the fixtures and fittings from the Pavilion and distributes them amongst her other palaces.

1849 A Bill authorising the sale and/or demolition of the Pavilion is brought before Parliament. Following fierce local opposition to the plan, a select committee gives the town commissioners (the equivalent of our council) an opportunity to buy the Pavilion for the town, at a cost of £53,000. A town meeting suggests popular support for this proposal and the commissioners publicly agree to go ahead, but many continue to argue against it. The dispute eventually becomes so convoluted and intractable that the matter has to be decided by a public referendum: Brighton votes to keep its palace by just 1,343 votes to 1,307.

1850 75,000 visitors *a week* take the train to Brighton this summer – 25,000 more than the coaches used to carry in a whole year.

1856 The construction of No. 13 Palmeira Avenue leads to the discovery of a Bronze Age burial mound dedicated to the remains of an ancient British chieftain. For hundreds of years the mound had been overrun every Good Friday by hordes of young people playing kissing games, unwittingly echoing the pagan rites once performed at the same spot to welcome the coming of the spring-goddess Eostre . . . !

1861 Hove now has over 9,000 residents, compared to just 300 in 1821.

1866 The West Pier is completed. At the opening ceremony in October, the Mayor of Brighton declares, 'the beautiful pier would [sic] remain as an example to future ages of what speculation had done in the nineteenth century'. Local conservationists object to the structure on the basis that the toll houses which flank the pier's entrance obstruct the view of the sea from Regency Square.

1871 Brighton's population reaches 90,000.

1883 Magnus Volk, the Brighton-born son of a German clockmaker, installs electric lighting in the Pavilion and opens the Volk's Railway.

1895 Herbert Carden is elected to Brighton Council at the comparatively tender age of 28. Carden, an unrepentant advocate of socialism at a time when many considered it the province of madmen, somehow manages to persuade his more conservative colleagues to join him on an unprecedented municipal trading spree: before long Brighton will have Corporation trams, Corporation housing, Corporation electricity and even a Corporation telephone system. Carden is also the first public figure to recognise the importance of Brighton's green belt, buying up large tracts of the land surrounding the town – as far as Devil's Dyke – and selling them on to the Corporation at cost. 'Take a little walk in imagination,' he will tell an audience in 1926. 'We have walked the whole of the way from the parish of Rottingdean right round Brighton up to the Dyke Road *on our own ground*. Future generations will say we have done something which I don't believe has been equalled in any other town in the country.'

1896 Volk extends his railway to Rottingdean with the introduction of the 'Daddy-Long-Legs' – a passenger car for 150 people on stilts 24 feet high. In the autobiographical *Three Houses* (1953), novelist Angela Thirkell recalls how she was never allowed to go on it as a child, 'because it had a habit of sticking somewhere opposite the ventilating shaft of the Brighton main sewer and not being moved till nightfall'. Many sources contend that this (no other word for it) contraption may also have inspired H. G. Wells to create the Martian tripods of *The War of the Worlds*, the first episode of which was published a year later.

1899 The Palace Pier opens.

1908 Edward VII (Victoria's son) stays for a week with his daughter in Kemp Town and, by all accounts, quite likes it. The *Brighton Herald* can barely contain itself: 'Nothing could have a finer influence on the fortunes of Brighton. Nothing could be more calculated to bring about an influx of rank and fashion to the town.' This last remark reflects the growing currency of the view that central Brighton is starting to look dilapidated and 'down-market'. In *Brighton: Its History, Its Follies and Its Fashions* (published the following year), Lewis Melville moans: 'Cheap excursions for "trippers" and half-guinea Pullman trains for the well-to-do have changed the character of the place out of all recognition ... Brighton has developed into the Cockney's Paradise, the Mecca of the stockbroker and the chorus-girl.'

1914 Britain is at war with Germany; on Brighton seafront, an Italian ice-cream salesman and a Dutch oyster vendor hastily redecorate their stalls with Union flags. On 9 September a French seaplane lands on the beach without a challenge because it too is displaying the Union Jack. The *Brighton Gazette* frets: 'It was all right under the circumstances, but many people asked what was there to prevent a German seaplane, carrying a Union Jack as a blind, doing the same thing? And if one could do it, why not twenty?'

1916 Brighton becomes a popular safe haven for Londoners fleeing the Zeppelin raids. The Dome and Pavilion are temporarily fenced off and turned into hospitals for wounded Indian Army soldiers. One eyewitness, who visits the encampment as a schoolboy, will later report: 'As some of the Indian soldiers got better of their wounds (a good many had arms and legs amputated) they wanted a little more freedom and so it became a familiar sight to see a crutch flung over the high fence and then another crutch, followed by an Indian soldier with one leg scrambling down . . .'

1926 On 7 May, and in the midst of the General Strike, a procession of striking workers is marching down East Street towards the front when 'a two-seater car driven by a woman approached from the sea. Seeing the strikers the woman must have stamped on her accelerator. At a bound the car leaped forward at tremendous speed. It literally ploughed its way through the body of the strikers. Several were flung to the ground . . . Men recovered from the shock dashed for the car, and some of them mounted the footboard. The police drew their truncheons and flung themselves upon these men . . . The constables dragged a man off the car, the woman continued to drive on at speed and turned swiftly up North Street. Who she is no one could say. She came within an ace of causing bloodshed' (*Brighton and Hove Herald*).

On 11 May, a crowd of strikers gathers outside the Brighton tram depot on Lewes Road to taunt the scabs/volunteers arriving to be trained there. Fifty mounted police and 300 officers on foot clear the area, forcing the crowd back to the Saunders Recreation Ground. When bottles and stones are thrown the mounted police make an aggressive attempt to enter the Ground, causing a near-riot. The *Herald* calls it 'the Battle of Lewes Road': 'The flying stones, the panic rush, the thud of blows, the shrieks of frightened women and children, caught in the confusion invariably aroused by violence – these things did not belong in civilised Brighton.' Once again there is no genuine bloodshed, however: just two policemen sustain minor injuries while a third 'had his trousers badly torn'.

1936 Scotland Yard's flying squad, working with Detective Sergeant Collier of Brighton CID, succeeds in breaking up the Hoxton mob, the last of the organised crime gangs who had been terrorising bookmakers at Brighton Racecourse with protection rackets for the last fifty years.

1938 Heinemann publishes Graham Greene's *Brighton Rock*, a story of murder, malice and 'milkiness' inspired by news reports about the Hoxton mob. The book is a popular and critical success, but many leading Brightonians take exception to its depiction of the town as a seedy warren of back streets rife with crime and destitution on the grounds that it will be bad for tourism. Greene would later comment, 'It must have galled them to see my book unwittingly advertised at every sweetstall – "Buy Brighton Rock".'

1940 Brighton is one of several areas targeted in Hitler's British invasion plan, 'Operation Sea Lion'. Beach landings are first planned for 15 September, subsequently rescheduled for the 20th, and ultimately put off until such time as the Luftwaffe could gain air superiority (the 12th of Never). The next four years of air raids will kill 200 Brighton residents and injure a further 1,000; 280 houses will be destroyed and nearly 20,000 damaged, although no building of historical significance comes to any serious harm.

1941 Herbert Carden dies; newspapers dub him 'The Father of Modern Brighton'.

1948 The Boulting Brothers' film of *Brighton Rock*, with a screenplay by Graham Greene and starring Richard Attenborough as Pinky, premieres at the Savoy Cinema in East Street (latterly the ABC, currently a gargantuan lager palace). Mindful of the mixed local reaction to Greene's original novel, the Boultings open their film with a disclaimer: 'Brighton today is a large, jolly, friendly seaside town in Sussex, exactly one hour's journey from London. But in the years between the two wars

... there was another Brighton of dark alleyways and festering slums. This is a story of that other Brighton – now happily no more.' The film is shockingly violent by the standards of the day and several national newspaper critics call for it to be banned, but the *Argus* strikes an uncharacteristically progressive note: '*Brighton Rock* ... has been described as bad publicity for the town. Those who raise these objections are the same people who prefer to attract the few and continually oppose plans which attract the crowds.'

1960 Construction of Sussex University (first proposed by Herbert Carden in 1911) begins at Falmer.

1963 Local garage owner Henry Cohen presents Brighton Council with a new plan for Brighton Marina, which he envisages being constructed on the seafront directly adjacent to the posher end of Kemp Town. A storm of protest from the Regency Society et al. predictably necessitates that this is changed to Black Rock, three-quarters of a mile to the east.

1964 On 18 May – a bank holiday Monday – between two and three thousand teenage 'mods and rockers' engage in pitched battles all over Brighton beach. By the end of the day, 59 have been arrested – for throwing stones, carrying offensive weapons (one enterprising young rascal was caught with a starter's pistol), threatening behaviour, using obscene language and damaging deckchairs (by chucking them at one another). The violence will eventually be immortalised in *Quadrophenia* (1979), despite the fact that it is rival resort Margate that ends up with all the knife injuries. (That film's heady vision of unfettered teen brutality is also somewhat undermined by Brian Lapping of the *Guardian*'s on-the-spot report: 'there was no difficulty talking to individuals, most of whom shared the desire to keep away from physical violence. The only boy who said he regretted that he had not yet been involved in a fight was speaking in front of several girls.')

1974 A major tourist survey finds that 22 per cent of visitors to Brighton are from other countries; in 1964 this was just 3 per cent. The sharp rise is probably due to the increasing abundance of English language schools in the town, as well as the growth of the conference trade.

The Eurovision song contest is held at Brighton's Dome theatre; Abba win with 'Waterloo'. The song subsequently goes to number one in charts all over the world.

1975 The combined population of Brighton and Hove approaches 250,000. After a seemingly endless series of consultations, proposals and counter-proposals, the Minister of the Environment finally approves a £100 million plan for Brighton Marina, including space for a cinema, hotel, nightclub and casino. Many continue to protest, not least resident tightass Sir John Betjeman ('No one who has the good fortune to live in Brighton will think that a garish pleasure slum built on the water will benefit the town').

The West Pier closes.

1976 The last cassion of Brighton Marina's breakwater is laid, but two weeks later the speculators behind the project contact the council saying they will have to charge an admission fee for walking on it, to go towards the £11.5 million needed for the harbour's completion. The council reluctantly agrees to stump up the cash on condition that the admission fee is dropped.

1979 The Queen opens the Marina as a working harbour on 31 May; it will take a further 23 years for Harry Cohen's dream of a 'city-in-the-sea' with cinema, hotel, etc., to be fully realised.

1980 On the night of 21 January a Greek cargo ship called the *Athina B* (*sic*) runs aground at Brighton beach, on the east side of the Palace Pier. It is unmanned, the crew having already been rescued by Shoreham RNLI after struggling for hours with rough seas and a failing engine. The wreck soon becomes something of a sensation as people come from miles around to gawp at, loot or listlessly kick it; the tourist facilities along the seafront are wrenched out of hibernation several months early and a great deal of unexpected money is made. When the day finally comes for the ship to be towed away (to a scrapyard in

Kent), thousands gather on the beach and wait for hours to watch. Unfortunately, the mist is so thick that no one actually sees anything.

On April Fools' Day, Brighton becomes the first major town in the UK to open a dedicated nudist beach. The move was instigated by Councillor Eileen Jakes (47), who famously helped her fellow legislators get used to the idea by bringing photos of herself sunbathing topless to council meetings. Not all were convinced, however: Councillor John Blackman predicted 'a flagrant exhibition of mammary glands', adding, 'I personally have got no objection to people showing their breasts and bosoms and general genitalia to one another. Jolly good luck to them, but for heaven's sake they should go somewhere more private.'

1981 Dan moves to Brighton!

1983 Brighton and Hove Albion reach the FA Cup Final for the first (and, let's face it, last) time, facing Manchester United. The result is 2–2 after extra time so a replay is scheduled, giving the people of Brighton another whole week in which to whip themselves into a footer-fuelled frenzy of self-congratulation. We lose the replay 4–0.

1984 The last night of this year's Conservative Party Conference (12 October) sees the Grand Hotel partially destroyed by an IRA bomb; 5 die and 34 are injured. The bomb was planted in a bathroom three-and-a-half weeks earlier by Patrick Magee, who received seven life sentences for the crime in 1986.

1987 The Radio 1 Roadshow, a travelling goon squad from the nation's favourite radio station, hits Brighton in August. DJ Gary Davies (remembered now chiefly for his smile-stopping 'Young, free and single' catchphrase) leads the charge by giving out free T-shirts and, er, playing records to a large crowd on Madeira Drive. For the first time in the Roadshow's history, however, the crowd is not at all receptive to Gary's oleaginous brand of charm and responds with abuse and missiles. The show has to be stopped early; a Radio 1 spokesman subsequently issues an official statement to the effect that the Roadshow will not be stopping in Brighton again – ever. I (DR) *know* this happened – I clearly remember experiencing my first ever swell of civic pride when I heard the news. Looking it up now, though, I can find no mention of the incident anywhere. Did I dream it? Am I mad? Or have I unwittingly stumbled upon *the biggest cover-up in radio history*? Do please write in if you know ...

1995 Julie moves to Brighton!

1997 Brighton and Hove Councils merge to become a single authority.

2001 The Queen (or, we may perhaps assume, an intermediary) awards Brighton and Hove city status as part of the 'Millennium Cities' programme.

2002 On Saturday 13 July, Brighton beach hosts DJ Norman (Fatboy Slim) Cook's free 'Big Beach Boutique II' event. The first Big Beach Boutique, staged the previous year, was considered a huge success by all concerned, attracting over 35,000 people and no trouble of any kind. A film of the show appeared on Channel 4 soon after, securing it semi-legendary status; an even higher turnout of up to 60,000 was expected at this year's rerun. In fact, 250,000 people flood into Brighton on the night, encouraged by fine weather and adverts in the national music press; 25,000 of them spend the evening trapped on the road between the station and the seafront. Nearly 100 are subsequently treated for crush injuries and hundreds more are unable to leave Brighton after the show due to overstretched transport services. Incredibly, only two deaths (one of them a heart attack) and six arrests are recorded.

On Sunday 29 December, a large part of the West Pier's mid-section falls into the sea. A spokesman for the West Pier Trust insists that restoration is still a possibility.

2003 On Friday 28 March, a fire destroys most of what remains of the West Pier. Fire Station Commander Phil Thompson tells the press, 'there is no way it could have started on its own', and rumours abound that a speedboat was seen idling near the structure shortly before the fire started. Council leader Ken Bodfish says, 'There was always going to be a substantial element of rebuilding rather than restoration. This will clearly mean far more rebuilding than envisaged.'

On Sunday 11 May, the pier 'catches' fire yet again; this time, all but the structure's cast-iron skeleton is destroyed. Fire Station Commander Danny Sherman tells the press, 'There were several seats of fire inside the structure itself – which is very unusual. If I was a betting man, I would bet that this one has been started deliberately.' Inspector Dick Shelton of Sussex Police says: 'At the moment we are keeping an open mind about the fire.' A spokesman for the West Pier Trust claims that 'the fire does not damage our ability to restore the pier to its Twenties appearance with significant usage of original materials and artefacts'.

2007 Time for the Timeline . . . !